OHIO STATE '68: ALL THE WAY TO THE TOP

The Story of Ohio State's Undefeated Run to the Undisputed 1968 National Football Championship

By Steve Greenberg
and
Larry Zelina

Director of production: Susan M. McKinney
Interior design: Michelle R. Dressen
Dustjacket design: Julie L. Denzer

ISBN: 1-57167-236-2

Printed in the United States.

Sports Publishing Inc.
804 N. Neil St.
Suite 100
Champaign IL 61820

www.SportsPublishingInc.com

■ ■ ■

For Annie and Rachel, who give me more happiness

and pride than a father could wish for.

Great football fans, they.

— S.G.

■ ■ ■

To my wife Lorie, my son Michael, and my daughters

Julie and Kristie. You are the motivation

and joy of my life.

— L.Z.

■ ■ ■

IN MEMORY OF

Doug Adams

Tom Ecrement

Tiger Ellison

Anne Hayes

Woody Hayes

Hugh Hindman

Tom Hauseman

Rufus Mayes

Brad Nielsen

Esco Sarkkinen

Vince Suber

(A portion of the proceeds from sales of this book will be donated to the

Woody and Anne Hayes Memorial Scholarship Fund,

which was founded and funded solely by the 1968 OSU football team.)

CONTENTS

ACKNOWLEDGMENTS

A project such as this doesn't come off nearly without a hitch by accident. I am in the debt of many for their assistance. For starters, my love, gratitude and appreciation go out to my wife, Sally, who proved once again to be the quintessential sounding board, a proficient editorial assistant and a pillar of stoicism in the "opportunity" of attending to Annie's and Rachel's needs (without very much of my help) as I wrote this book. Her steadying influence keeps us going. ... I offer unqualified thanks and appreciation to my co-author and friend, Larry Zelina, who embraced the idea from the start and was a wonderful, enthusiastic and enterprising partner. By the way, "16," you just wrote a book! ... The "fellas" from the magnificent 1968 national championship team were, well, magnificent. Those represented in this book made the extra effort and welcomed me, the outsider, into the inner circle without hesitation. Boys, I'll never forget it. And Baugh, thanks for sharing the folder of memorabilia your dad, Hugh, saved for you. May he rest in peace. ... My dad, Bob Greenberg, can now count himself as a contributing editor. We do. He helped tremendously with the research, and he has our sincere thanks. ... Sam Fosdick has that salient editing expertise, and he certainly proved it here. There's nothing like looking over that guy's shoulder as he's making his point. Doesn't stink. Thanks, Webster. ... Bill Mallory, a great coach in his own right, wrote a fitting foreword, and we salute him for that. ... Mike Curtin, editor of *The Columbus Dispatch*, lent us a huge assist in granting permission to us to use quotes from game stories written by Paul Hornung and Dick Otte. ... Karyn Smitson, my friend, colleague and running mate in grammar protection, stepped up with her insights and logic. ... Chance Brockway provided some great photographs for this project. Each is a memory. Thanks, Chance. ... Randy Baughn worked his digital photography magic for the chapter covers and player mug shots. They appear courtesy of Steve Snapp, sports information director for The Ohio State University. ... The staff of the Buckeye Hall of Fame Cafe in Columbus was most gracious and attentive to our needs. ... Our team at Sagamore Publishing couldn't have been more accommodating, especially "Mr. Acquisitions" Mike Pearson. Our thanks also to developmental editor Joanna Wright, director of production Susan McKinney, designers Michelle Dressen and Julie Denzer, publicist David Kasel, marketing specialist Jeff Ellish and sponsorship specialist Bret Kroencke. ... Special thanks to Sparky for the "fly" transportation, Little Tommy for the long-distance computer expertise and Bubba for the music. You boys always make it run smoother. ... Apparel courtesy of Sensibaugh Sporting Goods.

- Steve Greenberg
Carmel, Indiana
April 1998

During the course of creating this book, we did our best to put together a representative presentation of what I feel was and is the consensus of feelings and experiences shared on this team. Time and circumstances, however, made it impossible to contact every one of my teammates, coaches and support staff. But be assured, it is not lost on us that you all made vital contributions to our collective success. My respect and deep feelings for all of you have grown even more as a result of this effort. There is no doubt in my mind it was a team effort. I thank you all for allowing me to be a part of it. ... To my family, thank you for your unconditional support and understanding. This has been a unique experience for all of us. ... To my co-author, Steve Greenberg, whose passion for the Buckeyes is why this book came to be. We are tied together forever, my friend. ... A special thanks to Penny Harris for her electronic assistance. Your efforts made the distance from Carmel to Worthington nonexistent. ... A sincere thanks to brother Bob for your patience in letting little brother tag along. It made me better. ... And to brother Dale for enduring the inequities of it all. ... A reflective thank you to my dear parents, "Red" and Elsie, for your unwavering love, direction, and support. May you rest in peace. You are with me always. ... Last but not least, I thank God for all His blessings upon my life. It has been an incredible journey. Undeniably undeserved, but I am eternally grateful!

- Larry Zelina
Worthington, Ohio
April 1998

FOREWORD

Bill Mallory
Defensive tackles and middle guards coach

There were two important factors that contributed immensely to the success of the 1968 Ohio State University football team: the strong finish of the 1967 season (with victories against Michigan State, Wisconsin, Iowa and Michigan) and the freshmen players that year who comprised what was considered to be, and still may be, the best recruiting class in the history of OSU football. It clearly was a group that would make a strong and important contribution to the 1968 season.

Upon the conclusion of pre-season practice in 1968, we coaches knew this team had the potential to be a very good football team. We liked the chemistry of the team and its attitude. And we knew the key to this season would be our play against the third opponent, Purdue University, which had embarrassed us 41-6 in 1967. This was the Big Game!

Woody Hayes was at his best preparing for the so-called "biggie." Our preparation time for Purdue was ten months. We worked on the Boilermakers continually, right up to game time.

We had won our first two games of the season against Southern Methodist University and the University of Oregon, and now it was "The Purdue Game." With excellent preparation and great confidence on our side, we were ready for the No. 1-ranked Boilermakers. We were in total control throughout the game. The defense was outstanding in that 13-0 victory, shutting down their great player, Heisman Trophy candidate Leroy Keyes. It was a great team effort!

This victory against Purdue molded our team in a way that would elevate it to Big Ten-championship caliber. We would be challenged with our remaining games, but there was a confidence that we always would find a way to win. We did.

This team was undefeated after eight games heading into the season finale against MICHIGAN. We were looking forward to this game, and there was no way we were going to lose to Michigan. Our team so totally dominated Michigan, winning 50-14, that we indeed won the conference championship and earned the right to play the University of Southern California in the Rose Bowl. Great regular season: 9-0 and Big Ten champs!

Our focus quickly turned to preparations for USC and its Heisman Trophy-winning running back, O.J. Simpson. It was a tremendous challenge before us.

We knew that great preparation would again make us winners, so that's what we set out to do. As usual, Woody was at his best for this "Big One." Woody kept us constantly focused on the challenge ahead: beating Southern Cal.

The Trojans tested us early, with Simpson's 80-yard run for a touchdown. His big play did not so much shake us as it made us more determined to complete the task we set out to achieve. With that great determination, and drawing on the preparation, we took control and won 27-16. The national championship was ours.

We had achieved our goal to be the best.

The 1968 team, of which I was proud to be a member, was comprised of all the components that make a team, an organization or a business a true champion: great leadership, a commitment to excellence, belief in one another with great team unity and an attitude that spoke of never being denied.

Thirty years later, it is with great pride that I state here that we made a lasting imprint on the great tradition that is Ohio State University football.

INTRODUCTION

The 1968 Ohio State Buckeyes' national championship football season is a subject that has been discussed widely and documented thoroughly through the years.

The magic of an unbeaten season, the outstanding senior leadership and the talent-laden sophomore class each has been chronicled. So why did we decide to venture into this territory again?

Our first thought was to do something special to commemorate the thirtieth anniversary of that championship season and the team that made it happen. After all, it remains not only the last Buckeye team but the last Big Ten squad to win a unanimous national football title. And as outstanding as the 1968 Buckeyes were perceived to be back then, the magic of that season seems to intensify—and, in some cases, be magnified—with every passing year. The Buckeyes have come very close to winning the national title a number of times since then. And with each close call, memories of the 1968 season are resurrected, embellished, and sent to new heights of endearment by Buckeye faithful the world over. Were we, the 1968 football Buckeyes, really that great? Would we still be so highly regarded and fondly remembered had another Buckeye

team won a national crown since? It's all in the eyes of the beholders, but fate has dealt its hand and the 1968 Buckeyes will, in all probability, be remembered as one of the finest teams in Ohio State and college football history. As a member of the 1968 squad, I humbly concur.

It is, then, our mission to give you, the reader, a fresh perspective on the 1968 season. With the support and input of many of my teammates and coaches, we will relive the season through several of the guys who made it all happen. We'll take you to the practice field, into the huddle, onto the field during a crucial play in a big ball game and into the locker room. As we cover the season game by game, please join us as we reminisce about the memories that still are vivid in our minds thirty years later. Perhaps you will gain a keener insight of what went into getting us ready to play. Or perhaps you will sense the unity we shared while striving toward our collective goal. Or maybe you're just a die-hard Buckeye fan—like we all are—who delights in the opportunity to revel in the great tradition of Ohio State football. Whatever the reason, I hope you enjoy our trip into yesteryear as much as we enjoyed getting together to share it with you.

— L.Z.

PREFACE

The Official Word

Editor's note: The following news release (word for word) from The Ohio State University Athletic Publicity Office, dated August 20, 1968, will help set the stage for all you are about to read.

COLUMBUS, OH., Aug. 20 — Approximately 84 Ohio State University football candidates will report Friday, Aug. 30 for physical examinations and picture-taking proceedings with the required mile run also scheduled during the day. Practice will begin Saturday, Aug. 31, on a twice-daily basis.

"Woody" Hayes will be starting his 18th season as head coach of the Buckeyes, longest tenure of any football mentor here, a record previously held by the late Dr. John W. Wilce, who guided the Bucks for 16 seasons.

Having operated for several years with a dearth of speed and backfield talent, Ohio State fortunes are looking up this fall as a group of talented sophomores makes a bid for positions on both the offensive and defensive units.

To go along with a spirited group of newcomers will be 28 lettermen, headed by co-captains Dave Foley, tackle, and Dirk Worden, linebacker. Worden was the team's most valuable player last year. In addition, 15 other seniors, led by tackle Rufus Mayes, formerly a tight end, will be available. Mayes, like Foley, has started all 18 games as a sophomore and junior. He and Foley are expected to team as two of the best offensive tackles in the Big Ten.

Moving in with Foley, Mayes and Worden as two-year regulars are center John Muhlbach, defensive end Nick Roman, linebacker Mark Stier, middle guard Vic Stottlemyer and quarterback Bill Long.

Meet offensive tackle Dave Foley (70) and linebacker Dirk Worden (56), co-captains of Team Title. Their leadership was undeniably vital to the success of the team.

Rex Kern, the quarterback who had spinal disc surgery in June 1968, returns in time to start the season- and home-opener against Southern Methodist.

The 180-pound Kern will be sharing sophomore billing with several others. Jan White, a 214-pounder from Harrisburg, Pa., is slated to be the split end and Dick Kuhn, 208, of Louisville, O., is the leading candidate for the right side. Both are 6-2 and expert receivers.

John Brockington, 210, from Brooklyn, is a former All-American high school fullback at Thomas Jefferson. Blessed with exceptional speed, Brockington figures to start at right halfback. He was voted the best offensive freshman back. Three other sophomores rank highly among offensive plans. Leophus Hayden, 204, of Dayton, was an all-Ohio fullback but figures to be a halfback this fall. A sprinter and hurdler in track, Hayden has both speed and power. Larry Zelina, 195, of Cleveland, was all-Ohio and All-American in high school at Benedictine. Zelina, who missed much of his freshman year due to a leg injury, probably will do the punting and place-kicking. Another offensive star could be guard Dave Cheney, a 230-pounder from Lima. Cheney, who could be an offensive tackle as well, excels as a blocker.

Rounding out leading lettermen on offense are guards Tom Backhus and Alan Jack, halfbacks David Brungard and Ray Gillian, fullbacks Jim Otis and Paul Huff, tackle Charley Hutchison and center Jim Roman.

Lettermen returning from the defensive cast include end David Whitfield, tackles Paul Schmidlin, Brad Nielsen, Bill Urbanik and Butch Smith, linebacker Mike Radtke and defensive backs Ted Provost, Mike Polaski and Gerry Ehrsam.

Last year's freshman group, lauded by Hayes as the best in his career here, is ready to go. With all hands eligible, the group is intact, dimmed only by perhaps by a summer operation on quarterback Rex Kern of Lancaster. Kern, who won all-Ohio honors in football, basketball and baseball, underwent a spinal disc operation in June. However, physicians have indicated he will be ready for the season opener Sept. 28 against Southern Methodist. Kern, voted "most valuable" of the freshmen, netted 189 yards in victories last fall against Indiana and Pittsburgh.

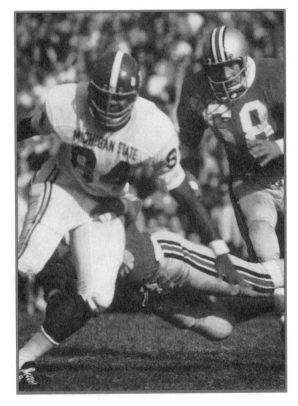

Jim Stillwagon (68) is a force to be reckoned with at middle guard as the season develops.

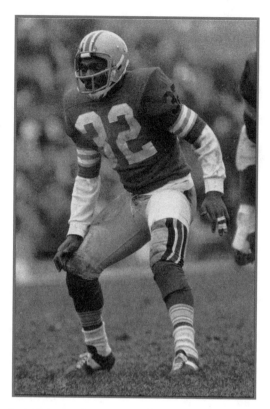

Jack Tatum, who was recruited as a running back, stakes out his turf as a defensive back for the Buckeyes.

Mike Sensibaugh, 187, of Cincinnati. Sensibaugh, who was an all-Ohio quarterback, made the shift to defense with ease, aided by his speed and ruggedness. In the opinion of the coaches, Anderson and Sensibaugh were the best of the frosh defensive backs.

Two other sophomores figured to help on defense are Doug Adams, 215, Xenia, and Mark Debevc, 210, of Geneva.

Adams is a fine linebacking prospect, who was voted the "best hitter" on the freshman squad. Debevc, who was a fullback-linebacker in high school, has been shifted to defensive end.

The varsity coaching staff has three new faces. Lou Holtz, an alumnus of Kent State, takes over as defensive backfield coach; George Chaump, of Bloomsburg, Pa., State is the new offensive backfield chief, and Rudy Hubbard, a halfback for the past three years, will be a cadet coach and working with the offense. Hubbard has not yet received his degree.

Coaches said he was the best offensive lineman among the frosh last fall.

The coaches believe at least six sophomores will help on defense. Middle guard Jim Stillwagon, 220, from Mt. Vernon, has been No. 1 at this position since the first day of spring practice. Stillwagon won 14 letters at Augusta Military Academy, where he played center on offense and linebacker on defense. Coaches voted him best defensive lineman.

John Tatum, 204, from Passaic, N.J., is an all-around football player. He can play either halfback or fullback on offense, and linebacker or halfback on defense. Tatum, who matches his speed with strength, was an all-New Jersey fullback.

Another defensive back will be Tim Anderson, 194, of Follansbee, W.Va. A fine tackler, Anderson also rates highly as a pass defender. As offensive halfback and fullback in high school, Anderson gained more than 2,000 yards in two years.

A leading candidate for the safety position is

Here's Mike Sensibaugh, a former all-Ohio quarterback from Cincinnati who also did punting for the Buckeyes.

A NOTE FROM THE COACH

Coach **Woody Hayes,** as was his custom, sent this pre-season letter to his players on August 19, 1968. This copy is from Tom Bartley, a linebacker and then senior-to-be from Springfield, Ohio:

■ ■ ■

Dear Tom:

Here's a recent excerpt from Sports Illustrated:

"SMU THREW MORE PASSES PER GAME (33) IN 1967 THAN ANY OTHER DALLAS TEAM—AND COMPLETED MORE (18.9) TOO. This was a needle in the pigskin of the Cowboys. In fact, SMU completed more passes (57.2%) than any pro team except the Baltimore Colts (58%). The Cowboys' record: an average of 29.7 passes thrown per game, 15 completed.

"Over 300 TV spots, 700 radio pitches and numerous billboard ads will follow the theme 'Excitement 1968.' Mustang Coach Hayden Fry is even sounding like an adman in his enthusiasm for the campaign, which he calls emphasizing the four E's — exciting, explosive, entertaining and electrifying."

There is one little catch to all this ballyhoo: they ain't gonna throw it if they don't have it — and that is the basis of our plans for SMU, for if we have the ball and are moving for touchdowns, we won't have to worry about SMU's passing. I have every confidence that our defense will do a

great job when they are called on. But I also have every confidence that our offense is ready to take over its share of the load. We've got speed, size and strength, plus another great quality — ability. For those simple but exact reasons, we will be able to maintain possession of that ball until we score. As I mentioned to you last spring, there will be times when we won't bother to huddle between plays. This will put a terrific pressure on the defense, but also a great pressure on us unless we are in perfect shape.

Every player that we have will be in better shape than he was in last year. I strongly suggest that you finish up this week and early next week real strong, and then take two or three days to freshen your legs before you report to us.

We will be living in Smith Hall, but Thursday evening, the 29th, a meal will be served in Baker Hall until 7:00 p.m.

Don't forget to bring your shoes back with you unless you want to practice barefooted. If you have any footballs, regardless of their condition, bring them with you for we can use them for the place kickers.

We will be looking forward to seeing you a week from Thursday, and be sure to come back ready for a truly great season.
Your friend,

Woody

P.S. A guy with a No. 15 passes pretty well too!
W.

DRIVE, DRIVE ON DOWN THE FIELD

Oh, that championship season.

For Ohio State University football loyalists, there hasn't been a time like the 1968 season since. In 1968, OSU completed a 10-0-0 sweep, winning the Rose Bowl over O.J. Simpson and the University of Southern California and finishing as the national champion. To this day, that star-studded team is the most recent from the

Big Ten Conference to have gone undefeated in winning an undisputed national title.

For Ohio State fans, it was a team of household names: Kern, Brockington, Otis, Tatum, Hayden, Stillwagon, Gillian, Provost, Polaski, Foley, Worden, Mayes, Adams, White, Whitfield, Jankowski, Long, Maciejowski and Zelina.

This was a time to savor; an unblemished run through the season gave college football

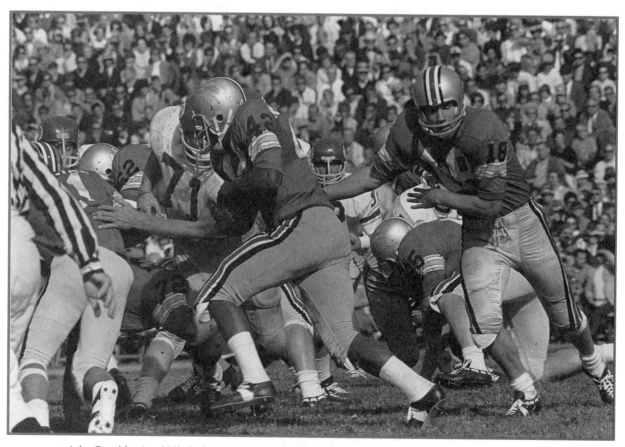

John Brockington (42) slashes through the defense. A gifted running back, he was in good company at Ohio State, where others of his talents would compete for playing time.

fans something to embrace.

There's nothing like a dominant football power to take one's mind off what was shaping up to be one ugly social and political year. It all unfolded in a cloud of marijuana smoke and an LSD haze, month by trying month.

In January, the Viet Cong launch a surprise attack on Saigon, the Tet Offensive. By March, villagers are being massacred in My Lai, South Vietnam. Senator Robert Kennedy announces his intention to run for president. Lyndon Baines Johnson, the sitting president, declares in a surprise announcement that he will not seek re-election. In April, the Rev. Dr. Martin Luther King is assassinated in Memphis, Tennessee. In early June, Kennedy is felled by an assassin's bullet in Los Angeles, demonstrators gather in Washington, D.C., to show support for the Poor People's Campaign and Helen Keller, the symbol of the handicapped, dies at 88. In a steamy August confrontation, National Guardsmen face off with rioting demonstrators at the Democratic National Convention in Chicago.

Not all was lost, though, in 1968. The brighter spots: *Hair* plays to rave reviews on Broadway. "Mod" is in, as are *The Man from U.N.C.L.E.* and *Star Trek* on television. The Beatles, Simon and Garfunkel and The Rolling Stones top the charts, the Green Bay Packers repeat their Super Bowl championship with a victory against Oakland and William Styron wins the Pulitzer Prize for *The Confessions of Nat Turner*. The space program is shaping up for the first lunar landing, the Cincinnati Bengals debut as an American Football League franchise, Detroit wins the World Series against St. Louis, and Pan American Airways and Aeroflot, the former Soviet Union's national carrier, open direct service between the ideologically opposed nations. Best-selling books are all the rage, too. Released in 1968: *The Electric Kool-Aid Acid Test* by Tom Wolfe, *Airport* by Arthur Hailey, *Soul on Ice* by Eldridge Cleaver and *Couples* by John Updike. And there is noteworthy progress socially as Shirley Chisholm becomes the first African-American woman to be elected to the United States Congress.

Piggybacking on the good news and providing salve for the negative were the Buckeyes. There was something about this team. Maybe it was the huge influx of sophomore talent. Maybe it was the blend of veteran leadership and the fresh-faced newcomers. Maybe it was that its time finally had arrived, a time that would make everything right in Columbus and other places.

Ohio State had won four previous national football championships. But this team really turned the modern era of college football in Columbus into a magic carpet ride and gave college football a shining moment. It rekindled the tradition, bringing Buckeye glory to the fore once again. Hang on, Sloopy!

What you are about to read will deliver not only the historical context of that season, but also the humanity of it. Pull a chair up to our table here in the Woody Hayes VIP Room in the Buckeye Hall of Fame Cafe in Columbus. Hang out with the fellas from Team Title. Grab a burger and a beverage, then get comfortable as you sit in on our sometimes-poignant, often-uproarious and thoroughly entertaining discussion of the season that was.

The players and assistant coaches tell you their stories of the talent, the friendship, the charity, the drive, the devotion, the knowledge, the ups, the downs, the tantrums and the caring of that championship season.

You're holding this book because you have an insatiable thirst for anything Buckeye. You can't get enough, can you? We hope you'll find this effort not only noteworthy but quenching.

College football, to many, is a religion—or at least a way of life. At OSU these days, about 93,000 people pour through the gates of venerable Ohio Stadium six or seven times each autumn to live and die with the Buckeyes. For many, that kind of fervor began in the late 1960s. It bears repeating: When the 1968 Buckeyes ran the table on the rest of the nation and ended up undeniably No. 1 in the major polls, they left the fans, players and coaches with a standard that has yet to be achieved by another Big Ten team.

- S.G.

CHAPTER ONE
The player's perspective

The foundation of the magical season of 1968 actually was installed during the 1967 season. The 1967 squad was coming off only the second losing season of Woody Hayes' coaching tenure at Ohio State. Still, many fair-weather fans were calling for Woody's scalp, even hanging him in effigy at the corner of 15th and High on campus.

But when you looked at the football situation, things were really not so bad. Although the Buckeyes finished the 1966 season 4-5, they were never blown out in any of their losses, falling to Illinois by one point, to Michigan State (which won the national championship) by three and to Indiana by seven. There was a solid group of returning starters in 1967 plus a very good 1966 freshman recruiting class joining the varsity. Don't misunderstand, there was a tremendous amount of pressure on Woody and the Buckeyes to produce during the 1967 season — or else. But the cupboards were not bare.

There also was the much-ballyhooed and highly touted freshman recruiting class of 1967 that arrived on campus that summer, and I'm proud to state here I was a part of it. Now back in the good old days, freshmen were not eligible to play on the varsity until their sopho-

more year. The freshmen basically were getting used to being away from home, adjusting to college life and its academic and social environments, and practicing against the varsity every day.

And practice against the varsity we did. It was war! Why? The frosh of 1967 only had two games scheduled that year, so for the most part the only competition we had to look forward to was in practice against the varsity. We would be the scout team, running offensive and defensive schemes of the varsity's opponent each week. We took our responsibility seriously. It was our job to give the varsity as good a look as we could to get them ready to play. It also was an opportunity for us to start earning our spurs, catching the attention of the coaches. We also just flat-out loved to compete, be it against the varsity or amongst ourselves. It soon was apparent that there was, indeed, was a wealth of talent waiting in the wings.

A love/hate relationship soon developed between the varsity and the upstart frosh of 1967. It wasn't an actual hate thing but more a wishing by the varsity that the frosh would learn how to better control their exuberance. There were days, then-junior offensive tackle Dave Foley admitted, that the big boys really needed an easy go from the frosh to get over some bumps and bruises, but the frosh rarely cooperated. And initially, that didn't sit too well with the upperclassmen.

It didn't take long for the varsity to realize, though, that there was some great young talent just dying to get the chance to join them and also knew deep down that by us going hard against them every day, we were making them a better team as the season progressed. During the course of the season, during the daily battles of practice, a sense of camaraderie and mutual respect developed, and by season's end there certainly was a feeling of unity and of purpose. There also was the 1967 season-ending, four-game winning streak, including a big final-game victory over That School Up North. A great way to finish, a great way to head into 1968. All systems go!

What you are about to read is the dusting off of tremendous memories of an unforgettable season, the glorious victories, magic moments and special team chemistry. Little, if anything, however, has been said or will be addressed in the future about the price that was paid individually, as an athlete, and collectively, as a team, in the quest for a championship.

It's worth noting, then, that more goes into winning football games and championships than just Xs and Os, or blocking and tackling. There has to be an understanding that each individual must do his part, whatever that may be, for the ultimate best interests of the team. Individual goals have to be set aside, yet each individual has to feel he has been given a fair

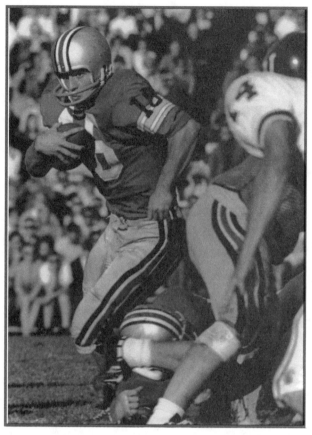

Larry Zelina finds the gap for the Buckeyes.

opportunity to compete for a position. (Ah, yes, that responsibility rests with the under-appreciated coaching staff.)

Consider this, though: There are approximately eighty players on a team. Each is on scholarship, and if he is recruited by a university of the stature of Ohio State, each was the top dog at his high school — if not in his region. Up to this point in his career, he has experienced only success, individual as well as collective.

All of that changes for some when they choose to compete for programs like Ohio State. The harsh reality is that, at best, only half of those eighty-odd teammates will get the opportunity to participate in games on a regular basis. And of the forty who do get a chance to play, perhaps thirty will get the majority of the playing time. That's a lot of broken hearts and dashed dreams for a bunch of great guys who are darned good athletes.

What, then, is their purpose? They sacrifice their personal dreams and continue to do battle, pushing the guys ahead of them to be the best they can be. They keep working and grinding, hoping their chances will come, and if they don't, they become the holler guys on game day, exhorting their teammates to victory. And when the day is done, you won't find their names mentioned in the sports pages or in box scores. But the following day you will find them at practice, in the team meetings getting ready to do whatever they can to make the team better. Are they satisfied? Not one bit. Are they an important part of the team? Absolutely. They are the heart of the team.

Consider, too, the ever-present threat of a season- or career-ending injury. During the course of the 1968 season, we saw a number of our teammates go down with severe ailments that would cause them to miss the whole season. A few never were able to step on the field again, their careers over. Still, they did what they could to help the team, most of them assisting the coaches at practice. They cheered those of us fortunate to keep our health, trying hard to mask the deep disappointment and frustration they felt inside. Were they satisfied? Not one bit. Were they an important part of the team? Absolutely! They paid the ultimate price for all of us.

There was a surly, stubborn old coach who used to tell us, "Fellas, there is nothing in this world worth a darn if it comes easy." And he was right. He worked us hard, but he worked himself harder. Spring practice, summer conditioning, the dreaded double sessions of summer practice, the pressures of the season, school, study table, you name it. We loved it. We hated it. But ultimately we did it. Together as one, as it should be.

-L.Z.

CHAPTER TWO
A fanatic's perspective

What did I know? In 1968, I was in the seventh grade and in my seventh season as a Buckeyes fan. There was nothing quite like an Ohio State football game. Still isn't. It was quite the deal for a twelve-year-old to saunter into junior high on Monday morning and talk about the big game played two days before.

I don't think I was in the seat at all for the home- and season-opener against Southern Methodist or for any of the home games. I remember stopping at the gas station with Dad on the way home after the Buckeyes had wrapped up that opening 35-14 victory. His car needed a fill-up.

"High test," Pop told the guy wearing the bow tie.

"Want one a these glasses for your kid?" the attendant asked. "Ninety-nine cents."

"Sure," Pop said, "A Coke, too."

The guy filled 'er up, cleaned the windows, checked under the hood, added a splash to the battery, made change at the driver's door, then came around to my side and handed me a bottle of Coke and a commemorative Ohio State football glass.

That glass became the repository for all my writing implements. It held court on my desk and I kept it, with its scarlet OSU looking back at me, for years. It was my souvenir of the season that was, yards ahead of all the game programs and stadium editions of *The Columbus Dispatch*. You'll have to ask Mom where it is now; probably in roughly the same place as my high school letter jacket: just east of Whoknowswhere.

That glass always was full as only glasses like it can be when you're twelve. At that age, there are miles between what you sound like you know and what you actually do know.

But to really know the numbers — on the jerseys, in the next day's box score and in the record book — was a joy of incomprehensible proportion. It represented the embryo of a sports fan, in general, and an OSU fanatic, in particular.

In the thirty years since Team Title went all the way to the top, hair has grayed, gravity has come to roost and service-station attendants have gone the way of their bow ties.

Still, the mere mention of the 1968 season sets a young man's heart and soul soaring to another time when all the news of the day didn't focus on guns and butter.

So, just go ahead and guess how I feel about the experience of putting together this book, the focus of which is the larger-than-life group of heroes of my pre-teens. They're mostly just regular guys now, sustaining and suffering the same exigencies of middle age we all are in — or are about to be in. Their conversation is easy and confident, something that comes with so many turns of the last page of the calendar, as well as the experience of doing something so right.

Tilt your head back. Watch the fading moon through half-closed eyes. This Saturday night in autumn has a hint of an approaching cold snap. You can still hear the 73,000 fans rocking the old Horseshoe. Ohio State: 35. Other guys: 14.

What a team, what a year. Dreams do come true for the true believer.

- S.G.

CHAPTER THREE
Meanwhile, thirty years later . . .

As soon as they walk into the Woody Hayes VIP Room at the Buckeye Hall of Fame Cafe in Columbus, Ohio, the memories begin to bubble.

Hugs. Remembrances from five years ago. Talk of Anne Hayes' recent memorial service. The stars and lesser-lights mingle like a family reassembled. Laughter and talk of children and of what everyone is doing now. Two guys share one set of eyeglasses.

The years have been kind to these fellows. Some seem to be in the kind of shape that would allow them to at least practice ... maybe for a little while.

We packed a lot into the discussions about the season that was. We had sought out as many players and coaches from that team as we could, and several threw in with us. Our idea was to pull from the roster a representative gang of stars, starters, backups and players from each class to help relive Team Title's rise to prominence. The cast, of course, read like a game-day program: Larry Zelina, Rex Kern, Mike Polaski, Nick Roman, Jim Otis, Bruce Jankowski, Bill Long, Phil Strickland, Dirk Worden, Dave Foley, Jack Marsh, Ted Provost, Jan White, Butch Smith, Jim Roman, Mike Sensibaugh, Bill Pollitt, Jim Stillwagon, Brian Donovan, Jack Tatum, Paul Schmidlin, John Muhlbach and Tom Bartley.

It didn't take long for the soul of this group to show itself.

Foley: I have only one artificial hip.

Nick Roman: Anything else artificial?

Foley: I wish ...

Long: Polaski could play guard. Look at this.

■ ■ ■

Some would call it nothing more than hamming it up for the tape recorder. Not this group. They used words and phrases like camaraderie, chemistry, love of the game, fear of a legendary coach. They had set their sights on a goal. They had worked hard to get there. They never entertained the thought that the success they all so desperately—and individually—sought wasn't possible.

To grasp what these men say today, you need to understand the culture of the Ohio State football landscape thirty years ago. Freshman didn't play with sophomores, juniors and seniors on game day. Those were the rules.

But the rules didn't say anything about practices. Tuesdays, Wednesdays and Thursdays were the days of fall where the recruiting class of 1967 began to be noticed. By the local and national media and fans, this group would be called the Super Sophs of 1968. To the upperclassmen, many of whom would lose their starting positions to these upstarts, they were a terrible lot.

There never was a time when they weren't trying to make a point—in practices, during two freshmen games or in the weight room. The 1967 season, at 6-3, was not quite near the standard. Under the guidance of a revamped coaching staff, these kids were more than ready to give it a go with their upper-class teammates to restore OSU football to its glory.

Their acceptance was not immediate, but as spring ball gave way to two-a-days in August, and then the regular season, a newfound re-spect had been hatched. The Buckeyes were a team ready to march out of the southeast cor-ner of the 'Shoe and make a difference.

Zelina: In 1968, there weren't a lot of se-niors, at least not starting, so what was the deal with leadership?

Polaski: Wait a minute! Let's talk about the change in the coaching staffs, from 1966 up to 1968. Harry Strobel was gone. (Larry) Catuzzi, too.

Zelina: Yep. He recruited a number of us.

Nick Roman: George Chaump came in.

Polaski: Yeah, you had (Lou) Holtz come in, uh, (Bill) Mallory.

Nick Roman: Earle ...

Polaski: Earle Bruce. There was a big changeover in the coaching staff, and I think that probably ... they say it starts at the top, and I really believe it did. I think that group of coaches did a great job of organizing and getting people pointed in the same di-rection. And then there was enough talent, you know, with the seniors that we had and a good

junior class, and *(points to the former sophomore class members in attendance)* you guys came along. If you went on and counted it up, I think you had twenty-two guys in the NFL off of that team. And there were another twelve or so that played either in Canada or what people would consider minor league football after that. So that was a pretty good nucleus of talent to work with. And you can see what the coaching staff did by just looking at their careers since that time.

Tatum: I thought Lou McCullough was a great defensive coordinator. I never felt like we went into a game where we weren't prepared, that we weren't better prepared than the other team. As far as his coaching methods, I thought he was about the meanest SOB I ever saw.

Marsh: I'll tell you what was great, more than all that stuff, was you guys (the sopho-mores) probably had more to do with the ath-letes who came here after you.

Nick Roman: I'll tell you what, though: We were inseparable. Day and night, night and day. You couldn't put a wedge between us. Anybody got on one of us, the rest of us would whup his butt. I mean, that's just the way it was. Not one person on that team segregated himself from the rest. That's chemistry.

Long: It's hard to say. Yeah, it's hard to say what comes first, the winning or the chemistry. I don't know. I really don't.

Bartley: The winning's got to be a result of the camara-derie. And how we put that together, people still want to know. Even in business to-day, you want to find that camaraderie so that your business works better.

Rex Kern (10), a fine passer, proves to be equally adept at running.

Nick Roman: I agree with you on the camaraderie, but you still have to have talent.

Bartley: No question. And we had ten first-class caliber coaches there at that time. Woody couldn't do it by himself. Now you guys have all seen teams that have much greater talent but don't have the camaraderie, whether it's at our level or high school or whatever. I was talking to a kid who was going for junior high school tryouts. And the coach, it was his first time. He didn't know how to cut kids. He asked every kid to write down four players that he'd want to play with. He said, "If you were a starter, who are four kids here you want to play with?" The worst player in the group was always one of those players. And the coach kept the kid because all the other guys liked him so well. Again, it's camaraderie. You play better together. When you like somebody, you play better.

Stillwagon: I think our freshman team had a lot of camaraderie. Many of us were the runts of the litter. I think I got the last scholarship at Ohio State because somebody refused. So Woody Hayes told me I got the last scholarship. I was just visiting, never wanted him to give me anything, but somebody refused and he liked me because I went to military school. Somebody told me they only had two linebackers, Dougie (Doug Adams) and myself and that I had to come, and when I showed up, everybody was a linebacker. And you had Lou McCullough *(he takes on McCullough's southern accent),* "Now, Jee-im, you don't come, we only gunna have one lineback-uh." That's Lou! ... I think when we went to spring ball (in 1968) we had a lot of camaraderie on our team. Everybody got along. Just like now, you're glad to see everybody. There was always dissension, but I don't think we had that much.

Zelina: Other than Strickland and Tatum ...

Stillwagon: And Harry Strobel calling me Phil Strickland all the time ...

Nick Roman: And I thought it was bad when he called me Jim Roman all the time.

Jankowski: This is kind of a strange analogy, but while in Kansas City, I came in the year after they had won the Super Bowl. There were some great names there—Lenny Dawson, Ed Budde, Willie Lanier, Bobby Bell—and they were a great team, but they were a much better group of guys. And that's exactly what we had at OSU. ... You'd give your life for these players, you still would. It was such a special group. ... It's amazing.

Foley: I think, going back to the transition (from 1967 to 1968) ... if you look at the guys that played as sophomores, it wasn't that we had leadership or didn't have leadership (in 1967); we just didn't win games. Our junior year, which I thought was kind of interesting, we kinda started off kinda rough.

Worden: Rough? It was the ugliest 2-2 you've ever seen!

Foley: And all of a sudden, rank kinda turned right there. I don't know ...

Zelina: I know that we were excited to finally get the chance to practice with you. It was a bear to practice against you. Spring ball was fun for us as underclassmen, because we had an idea of where they were gonna put us, but we weren't exactly sure. I mean, when we had our two games we ran a full-house backfield, and we had Tatum and Brock back there, and Leo was back there and I was back there and Jankowski. So we didn't really know what position we'd play in spring ball.

Polaski: The coaches didn't even know how the pieces were gonna fit.

Nick Roman: The one thing that I remember distinctly that was reinforced that year was that previous to that year you had guys—when Pork (Jim Roman, his cousin) and I first came here in 1965—who were going both ways, because they didn't have any talent (on the rest of the team). And they were just these big, lumbering guys that you just physically beat up. But then you got in a situation where that didn't happen anymore. You had guys like Timmy (Anderson) and Jack (Tatum). You know, Jack was a heckuva fullback on the freshman scout team, and he got moved over (to defense) because he wasn't gonna start in front of Otis, either. Now the defense began to get "athletes."

Otis: The freshmen, as far as the athletes, were the best group of athletes that we had at Ohio State at that time, even when they were freshmen. They probably could have played as freshmen, most of the guys in that class. I was thinking about that group, they were a little dif-

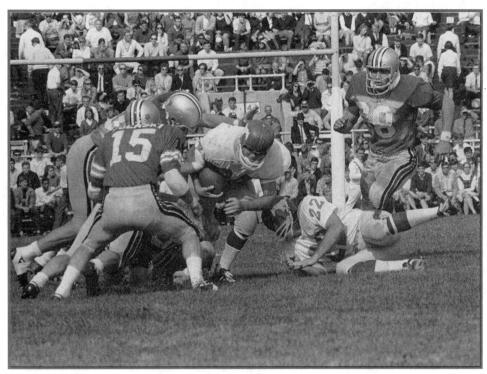

Mike Polaski (15), a junior, and Jim Stillwagon (68), a sophomore, put the clamps on another opponent.

ferent. ... I don't even want to say "cocky" but very confident, a little cocky. They were different from our class or the class ahead of ours.

Worden: I would say ...

Foley: And I've said a lot of the responsibility of our junior year really comes from the guys who were freshmen in the practices, because our practices were really heated up, you know? And then all of a sudden we started having a little momentum, and, I think, we beat Michigan that year ...

Worden: Big win.

Foley: It was a heckuva win, because everybody was really positive coming back into the next season.

Worden: The Michigan State game was bigger, though. Earle Bruce will tell you Michigan State was the turner, because ... Operation Constipation.

Nick Roman: That's right!

Worden: Earle would tell us ...

Nick Roman: That's right. The Old Man, before the game ... We kicked their butts. Well, we should've won the game before in 1966, and we're going up there, you know, in Spartan Stadium and everything, and Woody was really ticked off because two years prior to that they

held us to minus-9 yards rushing and buried our butts, you know with Bubba (Smith) and those guys? They were throwing toilet paper all over the freaking place. So Woody, before the game (in 1967), gets up and says: "Doggone it! This is Operation Constipation, and we're gonna stick that toilet paper right back up their butts."

Worden: We stuffed it right up there, too. That 1967 season really set the table for 1968.

Marsh: Well, that's what I wanted to address here. ...

Polaski: Really, when you think about it ...

Zelina *(to the upperclassmen)***:** When you guys came in as freshmen and sophomores, you didn't feel that there was a whole lot of leadership coming from the upperclassmen. And guys like Duke (Foley) and, I'm sure you felt the same way, that when you got to be upperclassmen and being a two-year starter that you were going to make sure the freshmen guys were comfortable, too.

Otis: Well, that's true. But when your group (the Super Sophs) came in, they were different. They had a hop in the way that they walked. They were not terrified of Woody.

Okay? I would say that our class or classes ahead of us had ... it was a little bit more of a reverence type thing, and would not disagree. We wouldn't disagree if Woody said, "Look, the sun's not coming up tomorrow." We would say, "Well, okay, the sun won't be coming up tomorrow." Your group was, "Are you kidding us? What the heck are you talking about?" That's the reaction your group would have had. I think that—and Woody would never say this—but I think if Woody had to go back and say which class did he get the biggest kick out of at midnight on Saturday night, he would have said your class because you had a lot of characters.

Zelina: There were ...

Jankowski: I remember coming in as a sophomore, nervous, but feeling I had a great opportunity being a starter on this team. But I was real nervous about my opportunities there and how good we would be. You're starting to hear about all these Super Sophs—that's how we were being touted. What kind of risk was there going with that many young players? I wasn't really sure. But at the same time a number of the younger players were coming in and replacing some fairly talented varsity players that were successful before that. So that tells you the potential. We were a very small team with the exception of Foley and (Rufus) Mayes at the tackles, but obviously with good quickness and speed. ... And speaking of the offense, when we were in the huddle—it's maybe we didn't know any better—but we just assumed we would be successful, and we moved the ball every time we needed to. No doubt whatsoever. We were just young and ignorant and we didn't know any better.

Zelina: ... We were told what to do and we

Junior fullback Jim Otis, powering through the line here, says the Super Sophs were not terrified by coach Woody Hayes.

did it. I think that was the chemistry of the team. Perhaps if we did have an idea or thought we were as good as it turned out to be, maybe it wouldn't have happened. ...

Worden: The best games were on the practice field.

Zelina: ... So we show up at OSU as freshmen. ...

Jankowski: Yes, we did, and one of the most rude awakenings I had was when we first met and we started running plays (and) I had to block. I had to block and I didn't know how. I never had to block in high school so I had trouble putting my head in the middle of somebody's chest. I remember Tiger (Ellison, the freshmen coach) keeping me out after practice to work on it. And I think I improved and became a pretty decent blocker, but that was one of the rude awakenings I had to go through. ... I remember practices as freshmen—be it in the middle of the field, or down around the goal line—we moved the ball successfully, we were successful all the time. And Woody would go nuts. We used to run plays drawn up on cards and move the ball. And I could feel the frustration of the varsity. But I just remember, just silently observing, this is a pretty special group of people. I began feeling this our freshman year, when we had so much success against the varsity. From no matter what position or what the condition was, whether it was running or passing, and I remember more running than passing, we had success everywhere. We really did. And you began to think, hey, this really is something special. And something that stands out to me—this was still as freshmen when they introduced our team at the post-season football banquet. They had introduced the varsity, then

Tiger Ellison started to give his talk, and part of the end of it, he's building about the freshmen, and his words were, "And the freshmen are here!" To me, that moved me so much. ... It meant something to me.

Zelina: So the only time we had the opportunity to compete was in practice, and so we (as freshmen) went at it hard, and we were learning the tricks. And Nick was beating my brains out everyday.

Nick Roman: Darn right!

Zelina: From the upperclassmen's standpoint, did you feel good about us? Did you ...

Foley: Heck, we hated you guys.

Zelina: David, why did you hate us?

Foley: Oh, man. The point was, you guys made us work harder than anybody wanted to work during the week and the bottom line was that class had more talent than any group of players that's ever come to Ohio State. In that one group. You forced us to be as good as we ended up being. I mean, you talk about going out to practice and saying, "Man I just played a game, and I don't want to have to kick my own butt every single day. I'd like to have a day off." And we never had a day off, because every day was another day of practice and each day we got better, because it would force us to be, probably, as good as we had to be. The bottom line is, uh, hard work doesn't hurt, but when you're doing the hard work, you'd like to have a day off.

Bartley: I know when we came in as freshmen, and then we were sophomores eligible to play, the sophomores took over the senior jobs. And the seniors did hate us. They wouldn't speak to us.

Nick Roman: Hey, Mike...

Marsh: When they ...

Nick Roman: Hey, man, shut up a second.

Marsh: I mean, shoot, these guys are wearing my butt out.

Zelina: Ski?

Polaski: The point was, you guys were good. A great class. The groups in front of you weren't chopped liver. I mean, like I said, there's people in that group that played professionally also. We had a lot of good athletes.

Zelina: Tremendous.

Polaski: And what happened was at that

point in time, a lot of times practice was tougher than the games, because you guys (sophomores) were trying to position yourselves to get playing time the following season. We're just trying to do our jobs, you know, and get things ready to play.

Worden: If the rules were different in 1967, we might've won the national championship if freshmen could've played.

Nick Roman: We may have won it then.

Worden: There was that much talent on the field.

Polaski: And it was talent that could play. When you go out there and you're practicing — and when we practiced back then, it ain't like a lot of schools do it today. Monday was the only light day. Tuesday, Wednesday and Thursday we were hitting.

Marsh: Yeah.

Nick Roman: You better believe it!

Zelina *(to Tatum)*: When did *you* get a gut feeling for what we had?

Tatum: I got it early on in the year because we used to have these drills with the (varsity) defensive backs. I don't know, those tackling drills that they had, I don't think we had a back that they could tackle in those one-on-one drills without us getting over the goal line. Guys like Rex, they couldn't even touch. At that time I knew we were going to have some running backs. I'll tell you who were the guys who really impressed me later on ... Jim Stillwagon and Doug Adams. When I switched over to defense, I used to go over there sometimes and they were over there killing people. I kind of looked at those two guys and said, "Man, we could have something here."

Foley: This team was really made in spring ball. That was one of the most interesting times I've ever been through. There was so much experimentation. There was so much No. 1 against No. 1, because there was so much trying to figure out where people were going to be, and all of a sudden, man, you're playing against some great athletes. ... We came out of spring ball that year, we all said, "Man, we've got something going here." And there was one thing I really felt we were going to do that next year and that was beat Purdue. I don't give a hoot what happened, we were going to beat them. We came out and our entire spring ball was focused on beating Purdue.

Polaski: And that was one of the objectives that was in the play book you got when we came back in summer. It said "BEAT PURDUE" — in capital letters.

Nick Roman: You guys really pushed us, especially the defensive ends.

Polaski: All the positions, with the exception of the tackles with you (Foley) and Rufus (Mayes), we played more than one person at every position. Routine. ... I still hate two-a-days.

Nick Roman: Two-a-days went so fast. It was a new chance to prove ourselves.

Zelina: I don't know what was tougher, the mile run or those ten one-hundreds.

Foley: The mile run.

Polaski: In season, it was full pads and full contact. I used to love Fridays. Fridays were my favorite day.

Marsh: Fridays we had no pads on.

Polaski: Friday was my favorite day, because you had helmets and sweats, you went to the golf course, you drove the golf cart ... ate big steaks, had pecan rolls. You take Tuesday, Wednesday and Thursday, man, and that was some tough stuff. I remember the defense talking about how many wind sprints you could do. I knew we'd run as many as (Mike) Radtke's stomach would handle. Then, we'd done enough.

Zelina: Was it the sprints after practice, or were the practices bad enough?

Tatum: The practices were bad enough and, fortunately, I worked more with the defensive backs more than I did with the linebackers because I was the monster

back. I was between the two and usually I warmed up with the defensive backs, which I was so happy about. By the end of warm-ups the LBs were dead. (McCullough) worked the heck out of them. But come game time, we were in shape and ready to play and we were always prepared.

Stillwagon: I think we just had a good thing. I mean, the upperclassmen, like Vic Stottlemyer. I can still remember Vic. You know, Vic and I became good friends. I walked in the room at Ohio State and I checked the depth chart and I was third string behind John Dombos at center. I used to snap punts (in high school) because I was a center, so I started snapping punts, and the first day I met Vic Stottlemyer I didn't like him because he knocked somebody out. He used to hit with a forearm *(he simulates with his own ample forearm and open palm).* And he said, "Bring some more meat up here." Vic says, "Yeah, I want to put another one out." And I was thinking, What a gem we have here. And then I got to be a center and ran down and made a lot of tackles. That's how I got to be a middle guard, and I

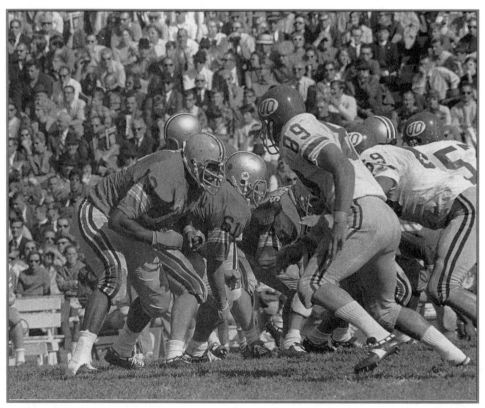

Offensive linemen Rufus Mayes (73) and Alan Jack (61) proved to be mainstays at tackle and guard, respectively.

was so happy when I beat him out. I didn't like him, and he didn't like me. But one day I was rooming with him on an away trip and I thought to myself, Man, they put me with this guy? And he turned to me, and I'll never forget what he said: "You know, Jim, you made my life miserable. You really ruined my life, but it's okay." And I go, "I was just doing what I was supposed to be doing." And we got to be the best friends after that. He said, "I had it made." And then that night he ends up explaining *Catch-22* to me, I mean the whole night until about four o'clock in the morning.

Zelina: The worst thing I ever saw was that 41-6 (loss) against Purdue (in 1967).

Long: Yep.

Zelina: Yet to see how strong that team was at the end of the year ...

Long: That's what I was trying to say. And it was a closeness ...

Nick Roman: I remember Dirk and I were walking down High Street with (Jim) Stillwagon. Wagon, a freshman, wanted to hang out with us this night. So we're walking down High. We see two, three guys walking at us, and we go, "Okay, Stillwagon, wanna be with us? Show us what you got." It was, you know, kinda like kids having fun. Wagon had the three kids tackled and on the ground.

Long: Maybe it was something like acceptance. Maybe we (the upperclassmen) needed to accept these guys to feel closer. Because we wanted to win, too.

Polaski: We were always together. I can remember being at the Rose Bowl, and Woody talking about our curfew: "Doggone it. We'll do it just like we did during the season. Be in bed by 10:30. ... That season, we could have held a team meeting at (the off-campus night spot) the Travel Agency at 11. Because there'd be anywhere from fifteen to thirty guys a week night at the Travel Agency.

Muhlbach: I remember the spring game (in March 1968) being a very good game. That was probably my first feeling that we had a pretty good football team.

Nick Roman: Figures. I got thrown out of the spring game because I punched a (running) back.

Muhlbach: It was a close game, though. Like, 24-21. Always before, though, one team just killed the other team.

Nick Roman: Yeah, because it used to be the first-team offense against the second-team defense ...

Muhlbach: There was so much depth on the team with the freshmen getting on now. The scrimmages were so good. ...

Jim Roman: It was too doggone early in the year to be getting our butts blasted by you young guys.

Otis: The group we had before the sophomores came up was a little bit more sluggish. When the sophomores got there, I think all play increased. ... I don't think that I can say that we were going to be the best team in the country, but I knew that we were going to be right up there in the Big Ten. I knew that we were going to be a good football team. Did I know we were going to be that great? No, because it takes more than great athletes and great football players to have great football. Unless those people gel, and we did gel, I don't think if you go through and ask any of those guys that came up in your class, I don't think they ever felt that the upperclassmen didn't want them as part of the group.

Zelina: Absolutely not.

Otis: That just never happened.

■ ■ ■

With the Super Sophs in the wings, pawing the ground like a thundering herd of horses, veteran players clearly had become a little edgy. In any group, everyone can't be the star. Nor, as the spring of 1968 unfolded, did veteran status count for much, either.

Everything became a mission. For the veterans. For the Super Sophs. For the coaches.

It all boiled down to change. And change, though it may be uncomfortable and foreign at first, doesn't have to be a bad thing.

Long: Some of our class played three years, and some of our class didn't.

Nick Roman: You're a senior and you got a couple of good quarterbacks coming into town, Rex (Kern) and Mace (Ron Maciejowski).

Long: Woody had to do it, huh?

Nick Roman: Yeah, Billy, but you scored

Quarterback Ron Maciejowski (18), looking to hand off to fullback Paul Huff (34), truly became the Super Sub whenever starter Rex Kern went down with an injury.

one of the most important touchdowns this freaking place has ever seen. Remember Purdue?

Kern: During spring ball, Kevin (Rusnak) and Billy (Long) played baseball. They were excellent baseball players, as was Mike Polaski. With Kevin and Billy playing baseball, that gave Mace and me the opportunity to take all the reps at quarterback. I don't know that Kevin and Billy playing baseball gave Mace and me a leg up on the quarterback position, but it certainly gave us the exclusive forum to display our abilities and talents. At the end of spring quarter my freshman year, I was diagnosed with a ruptured disc in my low back. This was toward the end of June. I had back surgery in July, and the very next month began practice. During this time, I didn't know—nor did the coaches or doctors—if I would ever play football for Ohio State. Pork, you and a teammate brought by a leg extension (machine) for me to begin workouts immediately after surgery.

Jim Roman: We brought it down to the barbershop (owned by Kern's father).

Kern: So for me, it was a matter of would I even play. In those days, not many players who had back surgery ever returned to play. But I put the pads on about August 15.

Long: The tough thing, guys, was that for some guys their career was basically over when you guys came in.

■ ■ ■

Teams of which the marvelous recruiting class of 1967 were a part went 27-2 in three seasons. A loss to Michigan in the season finale in 1969 and another one to Stanford in the January 1, 1971, Rose Bowl were the lone blemishes. Still, not many classes can claim better than a career .931 winning percentage.

There was a feeling among the Super Sophs and their junior and senior teammates that much more than the 1968 season title was possible. One even could assume it was expected.

Polaski: Hey! This is the only football team anybody ever talks about. If we beat Michigan in 1969, we win two consecutive national championships and would be, without question, the greatest team in a hundred years, and then you guys come back the next year with a chance to run the table. And this is the only football team anybody ever talks about.

Zelina: That's how spoiled we are. People ask me if I'm satisfied ... because we should have won three of them.

Nick Roman: Yeah.

Zelina: How lucky are we to have won one? But when you're talking honestly about it, we should have won three of them. No question.

Strickland: People ask me, What do you remember about your years at Ohio State playing football, you know? I say, frankly, the only thing I really remember are the two freaking losses.

Otis: Yeah, it's just too bad that we don't get to talk about the 1969 team, because we were better and we had one of those classic situations that you see in the Olympics all the time, where a couple of things go bad and we just couldn't get it turned around. As hard as we wanted it, we just couldn't get it turned around that last game. ...

Zelina: It was an awesome group.

Otis: It *was* awesome. What we had from the class was quickness, we had athletic ability, we had skilled athletes out of that class and I'm not just saying, you know, guys like you. I'm saying guys that played

on that defensive line.

Zelina: There were athletes all over the place.

Otis: Yeah.

■ ■ ■

Not every player in the recruiting class of 1967 actually played the position for which he was courted. Hayes and his staff had assembled a cadre of thoroughbreds. As a result, several positions were overflowing with talent.

That's why high school all-star running back Jack Tatum ended up playing defensive back, and similarly classed wide receiver Jan White was shifted to tight end. There were others.

Mostly, these guys just wanted an opportunity to play. Wherever. Whenever.

Jim Roman: I remember Lou McCullough saying about Tatum, "This is the next Jim Brown."

Zelina: As a freshman, Tate, you had a chance to see both the offense and defense.

Tatum: Yeah, I kind of switched around.

Zelina: You could have played offense or defense. How did you finally decide to get on defense?

Tatum: Well, there was a scrimmage when Woody took over. And it was third-and-one, and Woody told me to get a first down. "No problem, Coach." Everybody knew what we were going to run, either 26 or

Senior quarterback Bill Long (24) looking down the field for an open man, said the influx of the Super Sophs meant several upperclassmen would lose playing time.

27. Woody told me to hit the hole tight, so I hit the hole and everyone on defense was waiting for me so I bounced outside and went for about 40 yards for a TD in the scrimmage. When I got back to the huddle, Woody jumped all over me for not hitting the hole, and that's when I told him, "I play defense, too, Coach." After that, I started playing a little more on defense and then when I came back our sophomore year I had been drafted by McCullough. ... McCullough comes and he goes, "Well, we're going to switch you to defense, and you're not going to get your name in the paper very much and if you do it's going to be in the bottom line" and all this. He was trying to sell me on defense, but I always liked defense better anyway.

Zelina: Would we still be as close if we didn't win? Duke said he hated us, because (as freshmen) we never gave him a day off in practice.

Smith: Well, the only thing I can compare it to was when we were freshmen. We had the senior class of 1966 when we all got there. It consisted of first-team All-America Ray Pryor at center. And Ray ...

Nick Roman: Went downhill after that.

Smith: ... wouldn't let up for anybody. They used to have "cool it" days where they'd want the freshmen to really cool it, and if you didn't cool it they'd take you out. Some guy took my knee out one time, went after Mike Radtke's knee, see, because we were a little too aggressive, you know? I remember Rufus Mayes was the same way. Rufus would say, "Hey, let's cool it! I'm worn out, man. Don't make me look bad or I'm gonna hurt you."

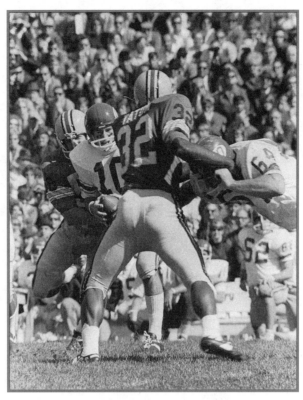

Said defensive coordinator Lou McCullough of Jack Tatum (32), who was recruited as a running back: "This is the next Jim Brown." Tatum, however, went on to become an All-American defensive back.

Smith: But when your class (the eventual Super Sophs) came in, they, uh, challenged everybody to do better. So, it was like the class was so talented I think what they ended up doing was pushing everybody to be better. And they didn't have much respect for the seniors. For instance ...

Nick Roman: Heh-heh. That's well said, man ...

Smith: ... when Strickland, a mean guard from Cincinnati, came up and in a full-go day on a Tuesday or a Wednesday hit senior nose guard Vic Stottlemyer in the (groin) on purpose and caused the biggest fight, probably in the history of the school, on the practice field. It was just a brawl ...

Nick Roman: There ain't no class out there ...

Smith: And I remember Bill Mallory and Lou McCullough smiling, you know? They probably were jacked, you know, because they were so excited to see this going on (during Michigan week) ...

Nick Roman: We beat those mothers, too, that year ...

Smith: ... it was like they challenged us, you know? There was no such thing as "cool it" days with that group—especially the kids on offense that were playing against the first-team and second-team defenses.

Polaski: ... Testosterone levels were fairly high on Tuesdays, Wednesdays and Thursdays.

Jim Roman: I know there was no going slow when Mallory was around, either. You had a guard or center over there against Stillwagon and Doug Adams and (Mark) Stier, and Mallory thought you were dancing if you weren't going full-go all the time. And I wasn't on the same level with those guys physically. I had to go full-go all the time or I was gonna get spanked. And if Mallory thought you were dancing ... He said, I remember, out at the Rose Bowl, Wagon was hurting, and he said, "Hey, Pork, just lighten up a little bit," so (I said), "That's all right with me" ... And Mallory says, "Would you guys like a band?" And I can remember to this day that he says, "I'm gonna start the music if you don't stop dancing." We're about four days before the ball game, and we start teeing off.

Kern: Pork, the maddest I ever saw you get, especially with me, was when we were practicing out at the Rose Bowl and the wives were coming in that day and I went to take a snap, pulled my hands out and you smacked yourself in the groin and you went down, boy. And I went, "Oh, man."

Jim Roman: About 10 days off, I'm all ready to go and Rex pulls out. Nice one.

Zelina: Bruce, when did the coaches approach you and give you the feeling you had an opportunity to play as a wide receiver?

Jankowski: Probably about a third of the

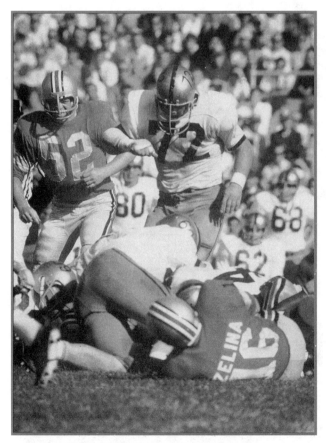

Center Jim Roman (52), looking to carry out his assignment, says it was full-go for the offensive line—all the time.

way through our freshman season — and it goes back to when we would emulate the team and the plays the varsity was going to play. They started to use me kind of at a split end type of position. And that's when — gosh, I don't remember if it was (George) Chaump or not — somebody said that I may see a position change and have an opportunity to play as a wide receiver. And I welcomed it simply because of the horses they had at running back.

Zelina: Yeah, there was some stiff competition there. But you know what? Our best attributes were our hands.

Jankowski: Yeah, yeah, I agree. And our versatility. ... I remember watching where Jan (White) was playing. I figured this was the guy I was going to have to compete with for wide receiver if he's going to be tagged at that position. So I began to see Jan being used more and more at the tight end position, which opened up the opportunity for me. Then I remember one time Woody coming to me and saying, "We expect you to be a contributor at split end." That is what we called it at that time. This was still before the end of our freshman year, which basically to me was more of a stake in the ground that, "Hey, this is your chance. This is where we want you to play." And (I'm thinking), I'll try to help the team. And I was elated. I was very happy that I felt that's where I'm going to get a chance to play at Ohio State.

Zelina: And there was so much talent there that you felt glad to contribute anywhere.

■ ■ ■

As Team Title began to gel, bonds were formed and respect was fostered in a number of ways — and not always on the practice or playing fields. If you went bear hunting, so to speak, you didn't need firearms; all that was necessary was a teammate.

Intensity rose as one of the hallmarks of this team. So did togetherness. There was no tolerance for much individuality where the team was concerned. And certain things were sacrosanct and remained unchallenged, regardless of whether they came from a player or from Hayes.

Worden: A part of the bond that developed over the years out of that program, and the amount of pressure that came upon that program in 1967, the pressure from the community. Those were bad times for Ohio State football. You look up and you see "Good-bye, Woody" signs flying around the stadium. I mean, go through a defensive meeting with Lou McCullough and you hear, "Why don't you guys answer these doggone things? They're calling for our heads." I mean, there was a lot of pressure thrown on that program. And to see it turn around ... in 1967 we started to turn it around, got that momentum going and all that talent, I mean, it was just, ah, it became a team.

Zelina: Speaking of "closeness," rumor has it that once upon a time there was a battle between Jack Tatum and Phil Strickland.

Tatum: Absolutely.

Zelina: Was that our freshman year?

Tatum: Spring quarter, our freshman year. It was spring fever. What it was, I was up in the room and it was a nice warm spring day. We had just come through a bad winter and it was just a nice day. And I went upstairs to take a nap. It was kind of warm so I decided to lay down in Phil's bed, because his bed was by the window. So I'm laying in his bed sleeping, you know, and there's a nice breeze coming through the window. I'm feeling pretty good. And all of a sudden, I wake up in mid-flight. I'm flying across the room. Strick comes in and takes a fit for me sleeping in his bed and flings me across the room. Woke up pretty quick trying to make that three-point landing. From that point, the battle was on. We start fighting. And it gets worse. We start fighting, and we lived on the tenth floor of the dorm. We're in the room and we're beating the snot out of each other. In the middle of the fight we stop. And we say, "Look, somebody's going to get hurt in this room. Let's go downstairs and fight." So we get on the elevator, go down ten floors out into the front parking lot and we start fighting again. The funny thing was, while we rode down the elevator together we were telling each other how bad we were going to kick each other's butt. So we go down there and finish the fight. The fight ends up, Strickland's laid out in the lobby. He's laid out on the floor and I'm going

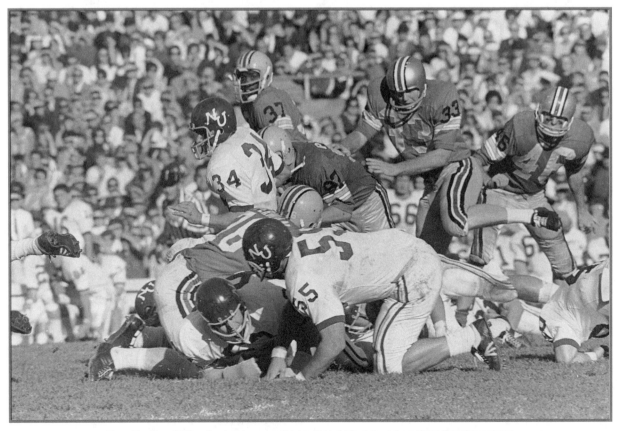

Tom Bartley (33), a linebacker, works to stand his ground against Northwestern.

up the elevator. My head's all busted up. I had to get eight or nine stitches right above my eye. Somehow somebody had called (academic coach) Jim Jones. So Jim Jones comes over and he doesn't know what the heck to do. And he says the first thing he has to do is take me over to the hospital, says we got to go down and get that cut fixed up. So Strickland jumps up and says, "You're not taking him to the hospital, I'm taking him." So Strick and I jump into his car and we go to the hospital. We were roommates at the time and we were best friends after that. It was just spring fever.

Zelina: Bart, you were active at linebacker. Anything stick out from the early days?

Bartley: I hit them all, but I knew which ones were the better running backs. And I'll tell you, Brock was something else. ...

Stillwagon: I remember one time in practice, my nose is split open, and McCullough goes (*using the coach's southern accent*), "Yeah, they we go. That's what we lookin' fo-ah. We gettin' it done, now." And then somebody starts throwing up, and he goes, "And that's the sound I'm lookin' fo-ah!" ... We'd be running, and Billy Urbanik would be down on all fours, and he'd say, "I'm gonna rip your freakin' throat out." And (Lou) would say, "Bo-ahs, did ya hear what he jest said? 'I'm gonna rip yer free-a-kin' throat out.' Run it uh-gihn."

Zelina: This is what I want to share with the readers—the people don't realize, all they saw was us winning. They didn't know how we felt or how we thought or how we were being treated or what it meant to us and to let the people know that the first couple games of the season, and probably the entire season, be-

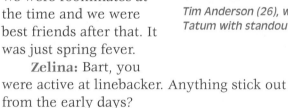

Tim Anderson (26), who impressed teammate Jack Tatum with standout play, moves in for the tackle.

cause every game was a challenge for us, that we were so intent on keeping up with other people on the team that we respected and thought more of than we thought of ourselves.

Tatum: That was the thing. We respected each other and we liked each other. ... I'll tell you, the guy that impressed me and one of the guys that made me want to play defense was Timmy Anderson. This was in freshman ball. There was a receiver on the varsity, Billy Anders, who was the all-time leading receiver. And we're playing and they had just brought the bump-and-run coverage in, and Billy couldn't get off the line against Timmy. And Woody got hacked off. So that was one of the things that made me want to play defense. The bump-and-run had just come in and no one was really sure of the rules on it and you almost had free reign to do whatever you wanted to at cornerback, so that appealed to me. And I liked watching Timmy Anderson. He was a great player. You know it's funny; I got all the publicity, but in some games I graded out at ninety percent and T.A. graded out at ninety-six to ninety-seven percent. ... The thing that I always tell people that I remember about the team is we had a lot of talent, but when we came in we were so young we didn't know how good we were. But the thing that pulled us over was that we liked each other. ... No, we didn't have too many egos. Like the guys that should have had egos— like Rex; he was as down to earth as anyone else. And the thing I liked about Rex, he wasn't a *prima donna*. He'd get knocked out and get up and try to come back the next play and run the same play he got knocked out on.

Bartley: You know, when I look at our

winter workouts that year (1968)...

Nick Roman: Ha! We threw a tennis ball back and forth.

Bartley: ... we played basketball more than we worked out. We would do our three required workouts ...

Jim Roman: Unless Mallory was there ...

Bartley: ... and then we would be in St. John Arena playing basketball. If the coaches were there, they'd play, too. We loved getting Mallory to play. I'm getting back to that camaraderie thing, but we got along with the coaches that well.

Muhlbach: Any of you guys ever play handball with Lou McCullough?

Smith: I did. I challenged him one time. Brad (Nielsen) and I had just come in second in the advanced intramurals doubles, and I was feeling pretty good and I challenged Lou. *(Re-creating the conversation with the high-pitched, southern accent:)* "Aw-right, Smith. Ah'll show yew how reeeeea-ly slow yew are!" He kicked my butt, too.

Muhlbach: We were playing Cut Throat one day, and Lou McCullough was gonna lose—and he pulled up lame.

Smith: Ah, geez!

Zelina: Does that surprise you?

Muhlbach: No.

■ ■ ■

Thus, through blood, sweat and a lot of laughs, the culture of the 1968 OSU squad was nearly formed. Chemistry? Sure. Respect? You bet. Take your fellow teammate for granted? Never. Were the coaches responsible? Perhaps. The players? A group of guys coming from all points on the compass? All keen competitors in their own right? Probably.

Kern: As freshmen, you couldn't play varsity sports. I thought that automatically molded freshmen together. ... That gave freshmen the opportunity to get to know one another better. It was freshmen against the world. We eventually became friends with the varsity, because we had to earn their respect. We did. It was a healthy and wonderful competition that we had with the varsity. That competition gave us a head start and a solid foundation for our future

successes as Buckeyes and teammates.

Polaski: But when you were freshmen, you couldn't "belong" and you didn't "belong."

Zelina: I think one of the things that amazes me was that there was so much talent there and so much competition, but, even in light of what Duke says, there weren't guys hating each other with all that competition. To have that many great athletes on a team and still be able to get along to me was the key to it. I mean, we were busting our butts, yet there wasn't a big head on the team.

Kern: There wasn't a petty bone among the group.

Zelina: No, there wasn't.

Polaski: I give credit to the coaching staff for that, because the coaching staff found a way to get a lot of people involved. They played a lot of people in different positions. They found playing time for everybody ...

Smith: Well, Lou Holtz was the master at that. I'll never forget one meeting he had with the defensive backs. We hadn't heard anything like that. When he said, "You all will have an opportunity to play," he was dead serious.

Polaski: He made it happen right off the bat.

Tatum: The thing I remember most about that year was it's probably the most fun I ever had playing football. I think it was just because of the group of guys we were with. We were having success but that was probably the most fun I ever had playing football was that one year, our sophomore year. It was unexpected, we were naive and young. We just kind of walked in with our heads buried. We had a ball.

Nick Roman: The thing I clearly remember was that we were together on the field, obviously, but off the field we were never out of sight of each other—or hearing distance—and so when you had a problem, someone else was there to help you. ... You messed with one of us, you messed with all of us.

Stillwagon: One thing about the team I can say is that everybody was different. I think that was our strength. We all ... had our own agendas off the field, as everybody knows. Everybody went and did the wildest things. Some were very religious, some were far to the left, but one of the things we all had in common was we all were winners. And when we'd show up, we played together. And when it was over with, we went our own ways. I think that's why everybody respected one another, because we still had one common thread: We were winners and we wanted to stick together. ... When it came to the team, everybody was unselfish and everybody played together. And I think that's what was so good about our team.

Sensibaugh: But back to football ...

Nick Roman: Football?

Sensibaugh: I don't think there was ever a point where anyone, or really Holtz and the coaching staff, was ever satisfied—with the exception of Tatum; he'd talk differently to Jack.

Tatum: ... I think Lou's thing was attention to detail. A lot of the things Lou taught us and we practiced under Lou we used the seasons even after Lou left. Holtz was a great coach as far as schemes and getting you in the right position and all of that.

Jankowski: Our skeleton passing drills with Lou Holtz. ... Once in a while, he had some shenanigans going—some kind of contest, a bet on something, that we wouldn't catch passes in a certain zone or something, pitting the DBs against the receivers. I remember that, and it was fun.

Zelina: It was fun and as good as that secondary was, I don't know what you remember, but I know we were still successful against them.

Jankowski: And they got better and we got better because we didn't go up against a better defensive secondary during the season.

Zelina: Still, Bruce, if you or Jan or I wanted to get open, we'd get open.

Jankowski: Sure we did. And if we had a good passing day, Woody would say to Chaump, if not to me, that we were going to pass the ball more. Then after the first completion of the game, that was it; we quit passing. But I remember hearing that, and after awhile Chaump would chuckle and look at me and say, "Right.". ... I remember another funny inci-

dent. It wasn't funny at the time, but obviously Woody didn't really care for stupid sophomores making mistakes. And there was a practice, and we were running Robust and sometimes I was in and sometimes I wasn't. But it was a blocking play and I made a mistake, and I came back the second time and made the same mistake and he started yelling and cursing, but he didn't touch me. I came back and made the same mistake a third time. So we got back in the huddle and Woody put his fist out in front of my helmet and rapped my head back and forth—left, right, left, right—about six times. I don't think I said a word; I was so scared. I don't think I ever made a mistake even close to that going forward. I really don't think I did. As a sophomore I guess you feared Woody. I did at that time, but through maturity and age your junior and senior years things change.

Otis: There was a big key on this team. It used to be that they'd put all the great players on offense. From the very beginning we had great athletes on defense. We would bend from time to time, but we never broke. We had guys that went to great heights on this football team. ... We had some great ones on the defensive side of the ball who could have played offense very well. But they were so devastating and so great on defense that that's where they played. ... And everybody had a nickname. If you went around and said, "How did we nickname this guy?" no one would ever know. I mean it would be hard to tell when that guy got that name but he probably got it for a certain reason. He probably got pounded on for awhile and then after that, it just stuck. I don't know when they are going to get another group like this together.

Smith: All I know is I remember spring ball that year was fun, because we had so much talent. We were so deep at every position that I think everyone realized that we were going to be something to contend with by the next fall.

50¢

Southern Methodist

Ohio State

CHAPTER FOUR
Ohio State 35, Southern Methodist 14

Take the mother lode of sophomore talent, put it up against a rifle-armed quarterback and an All-American wide receiver and brace yourself, right?

The Super Sophs launched their drive to supremacy by withstanding a 69-pass performance by Southern Methodist University's Chuck Hixson—who threw 15 of his 37 completions to Jerry Levias for 160 of his 417 yards. This one was a romp. It was the right way to start the season and get the confidence fired.

Five sophomores started for the OSU defense. Clearly, SMU coach Hayden Fry sought to exploit the fresh faces in the backfield. It didn't work. It almost was as if the Ohio State defense was daring the wily Fry to order the pass all day. He did, taking that supposed dare. Three of Hixson's five interceptions were grabbed by first-timers. All five picks stopped potential scoring drives by SMU at or inside the Ohio State 20-yard line.

The OSU offense showed an uncharacteristic—for that time—balance between rushing (227 yards) and passing (145). Three yards and a cloud of dust was not a theme Coach Woody Hayes was keen on for this day.

"We're becoming quite a passing team," Hayes said in jest. Remember, Hayes was the man who believed three things can happen when the ball is passed, and two of them are bad.

So, a little more than two months removed from back surgery, a 6-foot-2, 180-pound sophomore quarterback from nearby Lancaster began his journey to becoming a household name. Rex Kern had the kind of career-opener for which nearly any quarterback would pay. He passed for two touchdowns and ran for another. His 3-yard keeper was the first score of what would prove to be a magnificent season. He finished 8-of-14 passing for 139 yards and two touchdowns.

Halfback Dave Brungard led the Buckeyes in rushing with 101 yards. He scored on a 41-yard run and on 18- and 20-yard passes from Kern. Fullback Jim Otis scored on a 9-yard burst up the middle and totaled 63 yards rushing.

Perhaps lost in the impressive statistics of the two offenses was the overall play of the OSU defense. While the Buckeyes' offense struggled in the second half, the OSU defense ramped up its performance. As SMU was threatening to make a game of it, co-captain and linebacker Dirk Worden swatted away Hixson's pass on fourth-and-9 at the OSU 18-yard line. After an OSU punt, defensive end Mark Debevc sacked Hixson for an 11-yard loss to the SMU 23-yard line and, after a penalty pushed the Ponies back to their own 6-yard line, Debevc swooped in once more, pinning Hixson in the end zone for a safety. That all but wrapped up the season-opening victory.

A closer look at one play in the first half perhaps gave OSU faithful and the players a glimpse of things to come. The Buckeyes had the ball, fourth-and-10 on the SMU 41. Hayes called for the punt team to take the field, and as it did Kern waved off the unit. He ultimately scrambled for 15 yards and the first down, but not without first deflecting apparently solid hits while twisting and turning and keeping his

feet. It was a classic scramble. It was the kind of effort for which Kern would be known through three seasons.

What was more amazing about Kern's performance this day was the fact that in his first collegiate game, he called the majority of the plays in the huddle; that is, Hayes was not sending plays in from the sideline.

Hayes awarded the game ball to junior linebacker Mike Radtke, whose wife gave birth to twins the night before as the Buckeyes dispensed with the Mustangs.

The post-game huddle

Zelina: Before we get going, I remember Rads told me that Woody had called him into his room Friday night before the SMU game. And Marti was in the hospital getting ready to have a baby, and they didn't know until Friday night that the nurse thought that there was twins there. And Woody grabbed Rads by the shirt and said, "Your wife better not screw up this game for us." Amazing, amazing. ... Billy

Running back Dave Brungard (12) busts loose for a touchdown against Southern Methodist.

Quarterback Rex Kern (10), after waving off the punt team against Southern Methodist, begins his scramble for a first down on fourth-and-8.

(Long), I'm gonna put you on the spot, you had the toughest job of anybody on that team. As a sophomore, you led the Big Ten in passing. You were a two-year starter. How did you handle it, with Kern and Mace coming in? Share it with us? How did you handle it?

Nick Roman: He became obsessive with women.

Long: I didn't help myself by playing baseball and getting hurt. I was a senior and I would still do everything Woody would tell me. But in this game, we weren't up by that much and it was fourth-and-8 and Woody sent in the punt team. Well, Rex waves it off—and I'm standing next to Jim Roman and I say, "Well, here we go. We're gonna go in next time." So Rex called the play. They ran it from a full-house backfield. But it didn't work. Rex was back eight yards, and this linebacker takes a shot at Rex, and he scrambles and stumbles and staggers. And if you watch the films, and I have watched them *closely* … this is my life. Right now. He still hasn't gotten to the first down marker. Another (SMU) player comes across, and Rex is still staggering. Rex does a little juke step and goes right past him and off the field on the sideline for the first down. And, you know, from that day on … . From my personal point of view, I told Roman, "I've now got the best seat in the house." You know I don't want to put a damper on this, but for guys who are (used to) playing … . For me, when that happened, I knew I wasn't going to play.

Zelina: It was kind of a bittersweet deal, wasn't it?

Long: It was. That's a good way to put it. As an athlete you want to play, but also as an athlete you want the team to win. I really couldn't argue with the coaches' decision.

Polaski: It was an easy transition (to Kern) because we won. If we had been losing, it could have been real ugly.

Zelina: I understand that, and I guess what I'm saying is that if the quality of the people we had like Bill and Dave Brungard …

Long: Dave had a huge game this day, just huge!

Zelina: And you got guys like Dirk and Nick that got hurt, and they're just there watching. I mean, I didn't mean to put you on the spot, Bill, but it's really important that we bring out the adversity a lot of the guys had to face.

And still, you guys were a positive influence …

Long: It might relate to the other years (1966 and 1967) we were talking about. I think we wanted to win. We'd come from some tough years. … You just play game to game to win. (The sophomores coming in) was never an issue with this team. I don't think it ever would be an issue with this team. These kids … we wanted to win the game. But as Dave (Foley) says, winning helps negate a lot. When you win, you play a lot of players.

Polaski: We managed to put a lot of people on the field. And when we aim to run a hundred offensive plays in a game (like this one) …

Zelina: It makes it easy on the defense, doesn't it?

Polaski: Yeah.

Nick Roman: How tough could it be standing on the sidelines watching those eight-minute drives?

Tatum: Going into our first game … we had the defense all set and everything; my biggest worry going into the game wasn't whether we were going to be able to play. My biggest worry was would I be able to hold up with the rest of the guys like Cowboy (Doug Adams) and Wagon? I had been watching these guys in practice and they were like a machine, you know? McCullough had us so set that you had a spot to be at and you go to your spot and take care of that, and the next guy was going to take care of his spot. That's what you were worried about. You worried about taking care of your spot because you had no fear that the other guys weren't going to take care of theirs. I felt like I had to live up to the other guys and I think that was the beauty of what we had as a team.

Worden: I was so proud to be a part of it. To see this whole thing start to evolve in this game was really something. It was so

much different (than years before). Things started to come to fruition and you're gratified by that. And at the same time, my season came unraveled in one play against Purdue later in the season.

Polaski: When they came out in different sets, we had to recognize what set they were in. We had to know what four pass plays they favored in those sets, the four running plays they favored out of those formations. It was all covered during the week, so that when they came out, we put ourselves in the best situation to deal with it. And that was the easy part.

Zelina: How was Holtz on that?

Polaski: I will be forever grateful to Lou Holtz for the way he came in and took over the (coaching) position, because he took us from the Stone Age to the Space Age. He changed our coverages to the point where we played different zones. We had different "man" coverages. We played "man" with one free safety. We played "man" with cover-two. He made it very clear up front what he expected out of us. He just told us, "I'm the coach, you're the players, you play the games, we take films, we watch the films and I grade the films. If you do your job, you play. If you don't do your job, I've got six guys who can't wait to play your position,

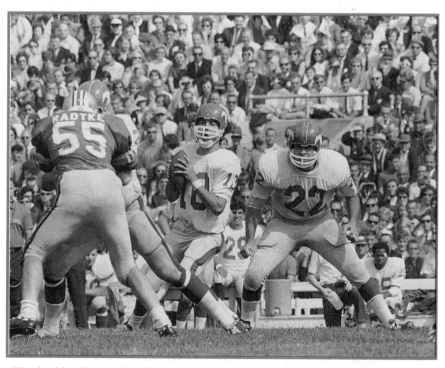

The day his wife, Marti, delivered twins, linebacker Mike Radtke (55) delivered against Southern Methodist.

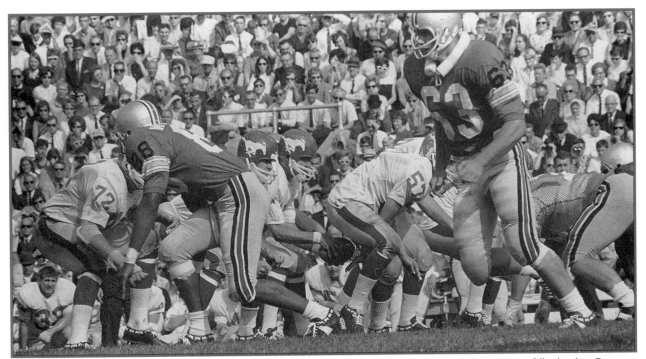

A Southern Methodist runner—as did others all season long—is about to take the full measure of linebacker Doug Adams (63).

and I don't care what your name is. I don't care whether your name is Jack Tatum, whether it's Mike Polaski, Joe Schmoe. If you're doing the job, you play. You don't, you sit." And that first football game, he made it clear, because Sensibaugh started that game at safety. I started at the closed-side halfback. Timmy Anderson was coming in and spelling me. When he came in and spelled me, I moved to safety and played for Sensibaugh. And when I came out, Timmy was the short-side and Sensibaugh was the safety. And I'd go in and spell Teddy (Provost) on the wide side. When we went to our film session, Holtz passed out the grade sheets (on the SMU game), and when he got to Baugh he said, "Baugh, I'd like to have given you a grade, but son, you weren't in any of the film." He said, "This is Ohio State University, son. Our safety man lines up twelve yards from the line of scrimmage and plays from there." He said, "You were so deep, you weren't in any of the film!"

Zelina: I think that goes along with what we said earlier, that the coaching staff on that team was just phenomenal.

Long: It was something special. There was a parallel on offense, too, with George Chaump. He knew the quarterback game. Woody used to insist on seven steps before you threw the ball. So we'd go, "one, two, three, four, five, six, seven, look, throw." The first time Woody did that in front of George Chaump, Chaump just about dropped his teeth. Chaump goes, "What are you talking about here?" And Woody ... and George tells Woody he wants the quarterbacks to throw from seven yards within one-point-five seconds and he doesn't care how they get there. ... There was a clear change on the offense, technically, and you saw it in this game ... what we were doing. We had a great offensive concept for every game, including this one. Whatever the defense ran, we had something for it.

Marsh: Just incredible.

Zelina: You could sense it was George's offense in this one.

Long: You had that ...

Polaski: I was watching film in Holtz's office one day, and Woody was in his office, which was right next door. And he's running film, looking at somebody we're playing who's gonna run a 4-4 (defense) and he was trying to figure out how to run 26 and 27 against a 4-4. Well, you got eight guys playing defense against seven guys blocking. You don't have numbers for you to be able to do this. Woody's watching and Woody's watching, and George walks by and he says, "George, get in here!" He says, "Yeah, Coach, what's up?" He says, "How we gonna block this, doggone it, doggone it, doggone it!" And George says, "Okay, I've seen this film. Run it ahead three plays." Woody says, "How we gonna block this, George?" "I've *seen* this film, Coach. Run it ahead three plays, because we're *not* gonna block it." And then, "What? What? What do you mean we're not going to block it?" Then, "Just run it ahead three plays." The team comes out, sets their offensive formation ...

Zelina, Marsh, Roman (*as Phil Strickland enters*): Hey! Hey! Strick! Hey, Strick!

Strickland: Hey, dudes!

Nick Roman: How's it going, big guy?

Foley: You're looking thinner ...

Polaski: ... So the team comes out and sets their offense. The defense is a 4-4. They put a man in motion. As soon as they saw motion, the defense went to an Oklahoma (formation). George goes, "We're not gonna block a 4-4, because they're not gonna play it. We're gonna put a man in motion on every down and they're gonna be in a "52" blackboard defense, and we'll run all day long." Woody would've sat there and piddled away the rest of the day trying to figure out how to block seven on eight. And George says, "Coach, you're not gonna do that. You dictate to them what they're gonna play. You don't want them to be in a 4-4? Don't let 'em be in a 4-4."

Long: The impression was BYOB—be your own blocker.

Foley: All I know is this game lasted until dark!

Zelina: It was a long one. I mean, they threw 76 passes.

Sensibaugh: The opening game, probably the biggest thrill of my life was running out there and hearing that

crowd. That crowd! That thing alone was just awesome, and it's also something that was never re-created.

Jankowski: And my stomach was upset. I didn't mess my pants, I didn't puke. But the butterflies were like nothing I had ever felt. And the sound. It was overwhelming. It really was. ... I was just happy to be there. I felt so proud and so lucky. Number one, just to be out there, but to be able to play and to have a starting position. It's a feeling that you could describe to people but I don't think people could begin to fathom what it's like unless you actually live it or experience it.

Strickland: The only thing I remember about SMU was the dumb ponies. McCullough would say (the defense) would wipe the dumb ponies off the helmets. ... We ran all over them. We kept the ball. The Old Man said we'd just run it. I still remember 26 and 27, could still block it. ... We just had to be aggressive with these guys. Hey! You practice like you play.

Marsh: I know one thing, and that's that they kept up under pressure with all those passes. There wasn't anybody standing around on defense.

Strickland: That Jerry Levias was all over the field! You didn't have any business standing around!

Phil Strickland (62) helps clear the way against Southern Methodist. "We ran all over them," he said of the 35-14 victory.

Zelina: Tate, in the game plan, did you have any specific responsibility as far as Levias was concerned?

Tatum: Only when he lined up on the wide side, because they always kept me on the wide side. We were playing a lot of man-to-man and bump-and-run.

Zelina: Any talking going on the field?

Tatum: No these guys were pretty quiet. I was surprised. I thought with him being an upperclassman and us being sophomores, he'd try to intimidate us, but he didn't. The thing about them was he didn't have any set routes. He just tried to get open. He was just running any kind of pattern. He'd run circles, go back across the field, he'd do anything to get open. I think they just told him to "get open and I'll hit you."

Marsh: That kept you alert.

Sensibaugh: I remember Holtz saying he was going to put a rabbit out (on the field) at practice and that that's what it was going to be like trying to catch Levias. But, seriously, Hixson was a back-pedaler, and every stinking time he'd pump the ball to the left—or he'd throw it to the left—before he'd ever throw it to the right. I got to start that day, and every time (he pumped) I'd react every time. I mean, he only threw the ball sixty-nine freaking times! I got my first interception. I fumbled my first interception; Tatum hit me. I had one in the end zone that I missed, or had my hands on that I should've gotten. I figured we were supposed to win the game, because that's what everybody said we were supposed to do. And I got benched afterwards.

White: Those were your fondest memories?

Sensibaugh: My fondest memories. ... Here we are, we win the game, I got an interception and Holtz is going through the (film) scores of everybody ... but I didn't get graded. And, as you said, he said, "Son, I couldn't grade you because I couldn't find you on the freaking film." And the next game, Ski started. Holtz was point-blank with me; I don't think he liked me.

Kern: The lead-up to the first game was all exciting! I roomed with Jim Otis the night before. Like Woody, I had a nervous stomach the night before games and would be in the restroom all the time. When Woody came in to say goodnight, Otie and I were in our beds.

Woody said, "Jim, we need a big game from you tomorrow. You also have to be a leader out there." Jim said, "Well, you know, Coach, if Rex goes to the bathroom one more time tonight I won't get a good night's sleep and you're gonna have to sleep with him for me to get my rest."

Zelina: Oh, my goodness.

Jim Roman: Oh, no!

Kern: Woody said, "By golly, Jim, that's not a bad idea." And then he said, "Just a minute!" And then Woody picked up the phone and called Dr. Bob (Murphy) and had him come to our room to examine me. When Dr. Bob was examining me, Woody said, "Dr. Bob, Jim needs his sleep tonight, because he's gonna run a lot for us tomorrow. Do you think Rex's gonna be okay?" Dr. Bob is winking at me as Woody says, "Well, maybe I should sleep with Rex tonight so Jim can sleep in my room. I said, "No, no, no. I'm gonna be okay." I slept in the room with Otis, not with Woody. What a relief!

Zelina: Oh, geez!

Kern: ... There was no way I was gonna sleep in the same room with the Old Man. So the next morning we get up—the quarterbacks would always have their meeting with Woody first—and we'd go into the room, sit down and talk about down-and-distance situations. And Woody would say, "OK, Rex, you're on the 20-yard line, first-and-10. What play do you call?" And we'd just go down the field like that. So we go through this and then we'd have our team meeting and our team meal, and the exciting part was the guys on the first team got on the first bus, and, uh ...

Nick Roman: All You Others ..

Kern: ... the AYOs got on the second bus. And you had a police escort down to the stadium. ... You're nervous to death and you've never played before a crowd like that. So you go out and you warm up, like Baugh said, you could feel the excitement in the air. ... This was really an opportunity for us to come out and play and see what we could do. At that point in time, you were tired of seeing your teammates across the line from you, so now you're excited about how we will stack up against that other team and other personnel. I guess the feeling I had was that we'd gotten so much talent (together) and it was time to play. But, really, the real feeling I had before this game was do I spend the night with Woody or do I spend it with Jim Otis?

Nick Roman: What a choice!

Kern: Yep, sure was.

Polaski: What made this game was the play Billy talked about earlier, when Rex waved off the punt. That won the crowd at Ohio Stadium. From there, he was solidly entrenched as *the* quarterback from that point on. Now, as I said, the guy who has a shot at a sack on him for an 8-yard loss on that play, had that happened, we'd probably have been looking at Billy quarterbacking for the rest of the season.

Worden: From a defensive standpoint, I think for the first time we came to realize, "Wow. Now we've got an offense." ... Just to score 35 points against anybody, it was one of the final pieces of our puzzle.

Polaski: And we found out we could play against any type of offense. It wasn't just that we could stop the run. We could now stop the pass. And back then, this was one radical offense. But for Chuck Hixson, the only thing he could do back then was just drop back and wing it. They had five guys who could do nothing but crack-block you. They'd just get in your way and give Hixson time to throw. All we did in the defensive secondary was basically just scramble our butts off. They caught a lot of passes, but we kept most of them in front of us. *(Editor's note: The huge passing day by SMU's Hixson wasn't damaging to OSU's chances. Most of it came between the 20-yard lines.)* ... Yet when you walked out of the film sessions, you'd have thought we lost. ...

Otis: And you just never saw that in those days. I mean a quarterback, first of all, didn't pass that much and second of all, didn't get that kind of yardage. But then, you know, we beat them pretty good and then we came back and played Oregon.

Worden: Jerry Levias took a lot of hits that day.

Nick Roman: They fumbled a bunch, too.

Long: It just seemed like we were a looser team.

Polaski: As Holtz told us as a group, "This is Ohio State University. We're gonna play great football. It's gonna be fun."

Strickland: Wait a minute! Offense was freaking fun! Freaking fun! Our goal was to stuff the ball down their stinkin' throats. We'd tell them where we were coming. That SOB across the line from me wasn't as good as I was. I told him we were gonna run the ball all freaking day long and do the same thing to him play after play after play. See? Offense *was* fun.

Marsh: I never thought we would lose. All we did was climb the mountain, one step at a time.

Kern: Prior to the opening game with SMU, Woody called me into his office, and he said, "Rex, I'm gonna tell you right now that you're gonna be our starting quarterback. And there'll be times on the field that you'll see things that the coaches and I don't see, and you've gotta go with your gut reaction."

Zelina: You figured you may as well test the waters.

Nick Roman: It's fourth-and-8 and you call a Robust formation.

Kern: It was a stupid play for the down and distance. I called Robust, fullback delay. Otis is to fake-block on the end, and Jim is the only receiver in the pattern.

Nick Roman: Where's the tackle go, the outside or the inside?

Kern: No, inside. A stupid call. But I sensed my teammates were looking to me to call a play. So we huddled up and made the fourth-and-8 call. Offensively, we tried to call plays as fast as we could. My challenge was to call a play quicker than Woody could send one in. Most of the time, it would have been the same play, anyhow. Except this time, Woody was sending in the PUNT TEAM! You've got to understand the total set of circumstances in this particular situation. It was late in the second quarter. We had been moving the ball very well. The momentum was with us. The defense was playing great. Why not take a shot on fourth down in this situation? The offensive team wanted to. Looking back, I would have called a different play, not Robust, fullback delay. But ...

Sensibaugh: I noticed when you went off the field after that, you didn't go too close to Woody.

Zelina: It worked, though.

Kern: It worked.

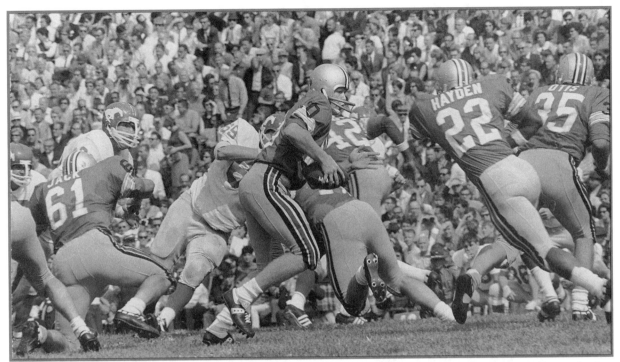

The offense, always moving quickly against Southern Methodist, explodes into action with Rex Kern (10), Leo Hayden (22), and Jim Otis (35) carrying out their assignments.

Zelina: Yeah, it worked.

Nick Roman: What did you think when

Woody sent you out and Rex waved you off, Baugh?

Sensibaugh: Mostly disbelief.

OSU vs Southern Methodist

SCORING

Southern Methodist   0   7   7   0 —14
Ohio State   14   12   0   9 —35

OSU — Kern, 3-yard run (Merryman kick).
OSU — Otis, 9-yard run (Merryman kick).
SMU — Fleming, 8-yard pass from Hixson
   (Lesser kick).
OSU — Brungard, 41-yard run (kick failed).
OSU — Brungard, 18-yard pass from Kern
   (kick failed).
SMU — Fleming, 6-yard pass from Hixson
   (Lesser kick).
OSU — Safety, Hixson tackled in end zone.
OSU — Brungard, 20-yard pass from Kern
   (Merryman kick).
Attendance — 73,855

TEAM STATISTICS

	SMU	OSU
First downs	27	18
Rushing	22-50	63-227
Passing	40-76-437-5	9-17-145-0
Total yards	487	372
Punts-avg.	3-41.5	11-36.5
Punt returns	5-1	1-17
Kickoff returns	6-75	3-32
Int. returns	0-0	5-15
Fumbles-lost	4-3	3-1
Penalties-yards	5-51	7-61

50¢

OHIO STATE

OREGON

Saturday
October 5,
1968

CHAPTER FIVE
Ohio State 21, Oregon 6

With nearly a full week of practice for the Purdue game behind them, the Buckeyes sleepwalked their way to a 7-6 halftime lead before putting away the lesser Ducks.

Jim Otis zipped around the right side for a 35-yard touchdown in the third quarter, and Ron Maciejowski, subbing for the injured Rex Kern, hooked up with Bruce Jankowski on a 55-yard scoring strike in the fourth quarter.

In the first half, safety Mike Polaski broke loose to block an Oregon punt attempt, caught the ensuing "infield fly" and ran nine yards for the score.

The OSU offense, although it gained 456 yards, was stymied time and again by the Ducks. Perhaps the absence of tackle Dave Foley, who was held out with a knee bruise, was a factor. Perhaps the Buckeyes were guilty of looking ahead. Regardless, four interceptions were of particular concern, including two which snuffed out potential scoring drives. One pick-off set up Oregon's lone score. Further, Oregon found enough starch to shut down the OSU attack at the Ducks' 41-, 27- and 18-yard lines. This one could have been a rout.

Kern went 11-of-19 for 113 yards and an interception before suffering a jaw injury. Bill Long had two completions, both to Oregon defenders, in relief. Maciejowski also had an interception, but its sting was lessened by the scoring strike to Jankowski to put the game out of reach.

The defense came up big again. Oregon managed only 140 yards of total offense and six first downs.

Fullback Jim Otis (35) streaks for the end zone against Oregon as tight end Dick Kuhn (81) provides the escort.

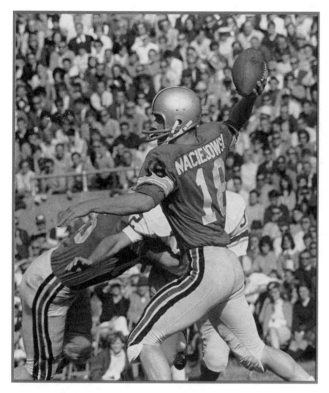

Setting up against Oregon, quarterback Ron Maciejowski (18) is about to fire a 55-yard touchdown pass to Bruce Jankowski to ice the victory.

Otis led all rushers with 102 yards on 17 carries and Kern had 49 yards on eight carries.

It clearly was time to begin practicing in earnest for No. 1-rated Purdue.

The post-game huddle

Nick Roman: How many times were you really hurt?

Kern: Who?

Nick Roman: You!

Zelina: In 1968, you were hurt, like, every single day of practice ...

Kern: Oh, man. That was a given.

Jim Roman: I had to practice, and my neck hurt so stinkin' bad!

Zelina: Rex and I had (hot)tubs named after us.

Nick Roman: Did you guys get any of the tape remover in there?

Zelina: No, but all I can remember is being in the shower and you coming in with that tongue depressor loaded up with that (deep heating rub) and someone always getting it up

the behind! ... See, Rex and I had it figured out. In the tub on Monday, sweats on Tuesday, jog Wednesday ...

Jim Roman: Sprinting on Thursday? Yeah.

Zelina: If you weren't able to sprint on Thursday, you couldn't play Saturday.

Nick Roman: There were some games we really had to put our head into ...

Worden: I thought going in we were going to beat Oregon ...

Polaski: It was pretty close to the vest for us. On defense, we had gotten ragged during the week just because of all the yardage SMU had racked up on us throwing the football. Woody was happy, but mad. That we won wasn't good enough. They used to their advantage every psychological edge they could get to make you believe that you still had to continue to work harder, and that the next team you play was going to be the best team you'd play.

Foley: Yeah, but on offense we practiced the whole week against Purdue's defense. We didn't even see film from Oregon. That wasn't even a factor.

Zelina: I think we spent one practice getting ready for Oregon. The rest was spent getting ready for Purdue.

Long: The offense didn't do much.

Nick Roman: The second half, I don't think they had a first down ...

Otis: The first three games, we made mistakes. I know that I had a big run against (Oregon).

Zelina: It was Oregon. You had a 35-yarder.

Otis: I'm talking about a pass reception.

Zelina: Oh, okay.

Otis: And I stepped out of bounds or something like that and I shouldn't have done that. It probably would have made things a lot better—it was in the first half and all that sort of thing—but it was just a stupid thing. We were all kind of making those mistakes and we hadn't gotten all of the discipline that we needed, I think, until about after we had gone through that Purdue game.

Zelina: Mace came in and threw a TD pass to Jankowski. They joke that it was the longest scoring pass in Ohio State history, Pole-to-Pole.

Jankowski: It was the Jet pattern, and I broke it up and scored. I'd like to have a dollar for every Jet pattern I ran in practice. And if you gave me a million dollars for every one I ran in a game, I'd still make more from the practices. The number of times they threw the ball to me was small compared to the total number of plays we had, but I'm not complaining. ... I've been asked if I ever thought about what it would have been like to have gone to another school and been the tailback. You know what? I wouldn't trade my experiences here for anything. I feel so good that I was able to contribute on one of the finest teams in the last fifty years of collegiate football. I think back during that time, sure everyone would like to touch the ball, carry the ball, receive more passes, but you are so excited just to contribute, if you could throw a good block on someone, you didn't care about the other stuff. A very unselfish group of people.

Polaski: Hey, on a personal note, this was the only time I ever scored.

Zelina: How did you feel about that?

Polaski: I loved it! I thought it was great. I thought it was gonna happen all week long ...

Zelina: You were the first player to spike the ball.

Polaski: Yeah. Looking back on it after thirty years, I'm sorry I did that. I was pretty certain I was not going to get back there again. Also, I blocked a punt that week, and I had been returning them. I said, "If you put me out there right now, I'm gonna block it and I'm gonna score. ..." It went just like we practiced it. Ran nine yards with my hands up in the air. He hit me with *it (smacks hands together),* BOOM! Walked right into my hands and it was a walk right into the end zone.

Jim Roman: I remember they had a

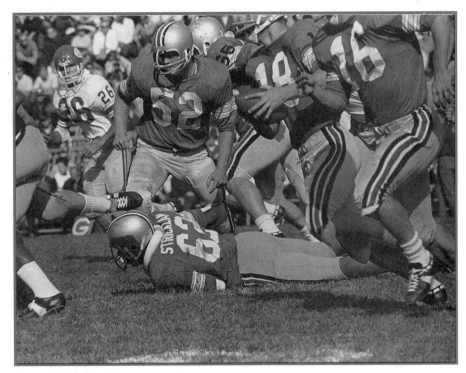

Jim Roman (52), playing with a neck injury, works at center against Oregon.

middle guard, something like 6-foot-3 and 195 pounds, who made a fool out of John (Muhlbach) and me. Johnny was slow, and I was even slower!

Sensibaugh: As far as the Oregon game, since you asked ... I didn't start. But I got involved in Ski's blocked punt. I can remember the Cincinnati paper stating that the only reason I was involved was because I wasn't starting. Why?

Nick Roman: Because you didn't have the *Zelina Plain-Dealer* writing stories about you!

Sensibaugh: But that was the first time I had ever squibbed a punt—in that game—and I came off the field and went over to Woody ...

Nick Roman: Whoa! Heh-heh-heh!

Sensibaugh: ... after he beat on me, he said, "Don't you ever do that again." I remember Earle (Bruce) getting with me, Rudy Hubbard getting with me, and they were saying to me, "Don't go off by Woody."

Otis: But that week (Oregon), he was there with the defense.

Zelina: Was he really?

Otis: Yes! ... I am sure Lou (McCullough) would tell you that Woody was with us that week. But Woody was down there with that defense. He spent the whole week down there and I am sure he added something and I am sure he got in the way. I'll tell you this much, Mike Phipps had played a heckuva of a game, (against) whomever they played the week before. I think we were all a little bit terrified of that guy. He just didn't do a whole lot against us. I don't know how much you've looked at what these teams were doing to us, but they were coming up and rushing us, they were blitzing us. That's what happened on this play (Otis' 35-yard touchdown run against Oregon). They all came up and I just flew by them. Had a big hole on the right side; the LBs were blitzing and the DBs were out of the way and there was just nobody there.

Center John Muhlbach (53), quarterback Rex Kern (10) and guard Tom Backhus (57) get ready to line up against the Ducks.

Zelina: Oh, I thought it was that great open-field running ability you had going there.

Otis: No, I might have moved a foot or two either way, depending on which way I was leaning on the handoff. ... But that was not a typical OSU game where we won on big plays. Generally our team didn't have to do that.

Zelina: And I think the Old Man buttoned us up, too, before Purdue because he didn't want to show too much going into that next ball game.

Otis: You know, we were vanilla most of the way but we were really vanilla in those non-league games. And then to have Purdue and they were No. 1, and of course they had Phipps and Leroy Keyes. Keyes could do anything; when he was in the backfield, he'd run to the open side of the field and use his great speed. ... We were having some difficulties with penalties and things like that. We were moving the ball.

White: We didn't even practice for these guys.

Jim Roman: Not that I remember.

White: Offensively, we were thinking ahead. I know we were.

Zelina: See, we could do it back then. Now it's harder for them to look past a team.

Jim Roman: The things that made it easier back then is that the fronts, the defensive fronts, weren't nearly as complicated as they are now. We didn't play an even-front defensive team until we went to Illinois. Everybody, these guys too, played a "50." Everybody we faced, almost, had an odd front. So we were practicing Purdue stuff offensively this week, spring practice, two-a-days. We never saw an even front. The Old Man wouldn't tell us that, though.

Smith: With Oregon, and from a defensive standpoint, you didn't have that much to prepare for.

Polaski: Formation-wise, it was what Purdue was gonna have. SMU would have been the aberration. They were going to be easier to prepare for because they didn't do some of the strange stuff that SMU did.

Kern: This game was a very businesslike approach for us. We were very thorough and methodical in our game plan. It was the Big Ten (season) opener the next week. Purdue destroyed our varsity and embarrassed Ohio State in our own stadium.

Jim Roman: And they spanked us the year before.

Nick Roman: Spanked!

Polaski: With Purdue, everybody on the defense knew this was the best team we were gonna play.

Kern: And as young as we were, it was hard for the coaches to come out and say,

"Hey, we're really playing great. We're a great football team." ... Our offense was overhauled, because of (assistant coach) George Chaump, Jan's old high school coach from Harrisburg. George got fired the first day he was on the job because Woody wanted to know if anybody else had any other ideas on how to run a better offense, and George said, "Yeah, we'll run the I-formation." And Woody said, "Heh! Like heck we'll run the I-formation. You'll leave before we run the I-formation. As a matter of fact, you're fired!" George says, "Hey, I've been here for two hours and I am fired before I get started."

Zelina: But we did end up running the "I."

Kern: We did. The Rip and Liz. I-formation allowed us many options, including passing, on first down our sophomore year. We're throwing a 3-yard pass like Mace threw to Bruce Jankowski that ended up being a 55-yard touchdown pass in this game. That, historically, had not been Ohio State football. ... But still, we were motivated. Let me tell you.

Zelina: It was easy for Woody to motivate us, but by the time we were seniors the stuff we'd been hearing for two years was old. But still, it had a tremendous impact on us for this game and the rest that followed it, including Purdue.

Bill Urbanik (79) does his job as the defense limits Oregon to just six downs.

OSU vs Oregon

SCORING

Oregon	0	6	0	0	— 6
Ohio State	7	0	7	7	—21

OSU — Polaski, 9-yard return of blocked punt (Merryman kick).

ORE — Schuler , 10-yard pass from Harrington (kick failed).

OSU — Otis, 35-yard run (Merryman kick).

OSU — Jankowski, 55-yard pass from Maciejowski (Merryman kick).

Attendance — 70,191

TEAM STATISTICS

	ORE	OSU
First downs	6	22
Rushing	41-62	70-288
Passing	8-21-78-2	12-25-168-4
Total yards	140	456
Punts-avg.	13-39	5-36.8
Punt returns	0-0	6-77
Kickoff returns	4-49	1-14
Int. returns	4-38	1-14
Fumbles-lost	3-1	3-2
Penalties-yards	1-5	3-33

SALUTE TO THE 1968 OLYMPICS
MEXICO CITY

PURDUE   **OHIO STATE**

OCTOBER 12, 1968 · OFFICIAL PROGRAM · FIFTY CENTS

CHAPTER SIX
Ohio State 13, Purdue 0

Coach Woody Hayes had the No. 1-ranked Boilermakers in his sights since his team had suffered that humiliating 41-6 thrashing in Columbus the previous season. He made no bones about it, either; Purdue was going down one way or another.

Before a then-record Ohio Stadium crowd of 84,834, the top-rated Boilermaker Express was more than derailed by No. 5 OSU; it nearly was humiliated by the Buckeyes, who featured nine sophomore starters and five more who played significant minutes.

Purdue entered the game averaging more than 40 points a game with All-America quarterback Mike Phipps ("No. 15"—remember Woody's letter?) and Heisman Trophy front-runner Leroy Keyes, a versatile two-way performer at halfback and cornerback. All Purdue got for its notoriety and efforts: 186 total yards. Keyes contributed 19 rushing yards on seven carries and had four receptions for 44 yards. Bye, bye No. 1. Bye, bye Heisman.

"I think Woody out-coached me," Purdue Coach Jack Mollenkopf said. "... They were higher emotionally than we were."

To be sure, Hayes had his players primed.

After a scoreless first half—Purdue's lone first-half shutout in twenty-eight games and one during which OSU repeatedly cost itself scoring chances by missing three field-goal attempts and committing fumbles and penalties—the game literally was decided in the third quarter, when Buckeyes safety Ted Provost stepped in front of a Phipps pass in the flat, picked it off and raced 34 yards southward down the sun-splashed west sideline.

"I was scared of those 'flat' passes," Mollenkopf said. "We hadn't thrown long (by that point in the game). Maybe if we had, we could have kept (Provost) back there."

This game was iced by quarterback Bill Long's 14-yard scoring run, one many still consider to be the most crucial in OSU's vaunted history. Playing in place of Rex Kern, who became sidelined with an injured wrist only one play before, Long dropped back to pass but spotted a lane up the middle. He pulled the ball down, tucked it away and headed for the goal line, meeting up with a pair of Boilermakers defenders at the 2-yard line and dragging them into the end zone.

The Buckeyes' offense was absolutely relentless, pounding away at the supposedly superior Boilermakers' defense for 333 total yards. "I knew we could run against them," Hayes said.

Fullback Jim Otis led the way with 29 carries for 144 yards, halfback John Brockington had 10 carries for 69 yards, quarterback Rex Kern had 11 carries for 45 yards and halfback Dave Brungard had 10 carries for 41 yards. There was no answer readily available from across the field.

"The four coaches and the starters, they did it," Hayes said. "I don't coach defense at all anymore. ... Jack Tatum covered Keyes so well. Tatum just has great quickness and the ability to recover."

Phipps struggled to a 10-of-28, 120-yard outing and had a second interception, this time by middle guard Jim Stillwagon, who stepped in front of a short toss at the Boilermakers' 26-yard line. Five plays later, Long's TD all but slammed the door on any hopes for a Purdue victory.

Said Hayes: "(Phipps) has said he can read his patterns better this year. Well, our kids didn't give him much time to read. He was on the seat of his pants quite often."

Perhaps an alert fourth-quarter play by linebacker Doug Adams was all the insurance OSU needed. With fourth-and-goal at the OSU 7-yard line, Adams tipped a pass intended for Keyes. The ball continued its path toward the intended receiver, but cornerback Tim Anderson was there to make certain Keyes had no chance at it.

"Let me say this without equivocation: That was the greatest defensive effort I have ever, ever seen," Hayes said. "It was unbelievable what they did to a great football team. I take nothing away from Purdue. Study their movies and you can see what they can do with the football. I just can't believe the job our defense did. ... I can't remember a greater victory. No defensive effort ever came close to this. ... Purdue had first-and-goal at our 7-yard line and ended up on the 7-yard line. That's great defense."

The post-game huddle

Tatum: I think for that game we had a great game plan because the things that Purdue did, they weren't very complicated but they did

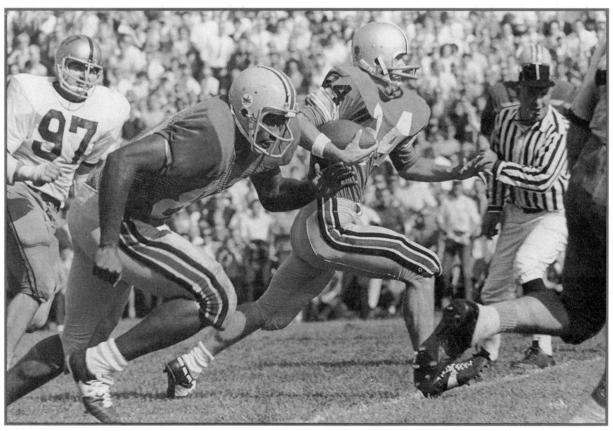

Bill Long (24) subs at quarterback for Rex Kern against Purdue—and heads for the end zone.

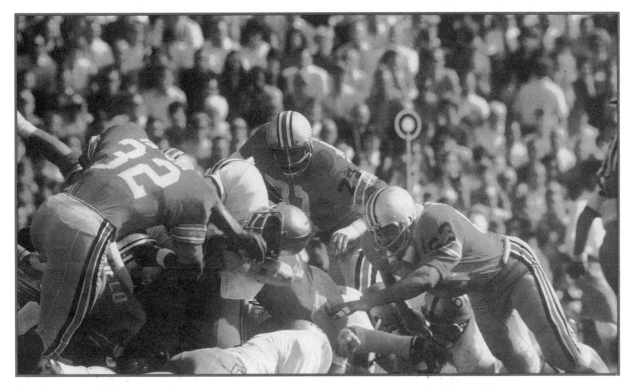

Defensive back Jack Tatum (32) makes certain the Purdue ball carrier isn't going anywhere.

them very well. And when Keyes was in the backfield, they were going to run the toss sweep. When he was in the backfield, I kind of moved in and either blitzed or made sure they didn't get around the outside on the run. When Keyes split out I just covered him man on man. I think cutting off the running game was the big deal. That's what we had to do. We couldn't let him get into a rhythm in that running game.

Otis: You know, you look back, we made ... here is how I recall this game. We really played a much better game against Purdue. I don't know what we were rated but we were in the Top Ten someplace and they were No. 1. But, we really outplayed these guys. I mean, we made a lot of mistakes ... we made mistakes in our first three games. It wasn't until we played Northwestern, who was kind of a mediocre Big Ten team, that we just dominated there. ... The defense probably played a better game—mistake free—than we did because we were making silly mistakes that you do on offense when you're not as disciplined as you need to be.

Zelina: Well, in the first quarter ... the first and second quarters when we kept driving

down to their end of the field, we had a holding penalty. I looked at the highlight film and there were three big plays that we made in a row that were called back because of penalties and we wound up with nothing.

Otis: Yeah.

Zelina: And despite that, the defense ... whoa, what a game that was, boy!

Otis: You know? They were great players.

Foley: *The* play, to be real honest with you, was Billy Long's play. That actually put the whole season into perspective, because, again, you got a guy coming in cold turkey and he puts the other points on the board. I'd say that kinda set the stage for the whole season.

Nick Roman: Was that third down, Bill?

Long: Yeah.

Zelina: Can you talk about it?

Long: Woody called a hitch pass to Jan White. It was the 99-Hitch. I remember going back (in the pocket) and seeing the linebacker, in my first three steps, sitting on Jan, and I knew it was not going to work. ... So I thought, I'm in trouble here. And then it was like a truck went through there; the line opened up. The defensive back was in the end zone, and he stayed in the end zone. I went right to his feet.

Zelina: It was like slow motion getting there, wasn't it?

Long: Yeah, well ...

Marsh: Look, there's Billy with his high-tops on.

Long: It felt like it took forever, but it didn't. But the significant thing was that we were only up 6-0 before that play.

Zelina: That was the turning point. ... Man, I remember how intense it was that week. The coaching staff was just absolutely freaking intense!

Long: And they didn't want us to peak too early. By Monday we were sky high!

Foley: And I'll tell you something else that's worth mentioning as far as offensive innovation, and this goes back to what they did on defense. The whole time, from when we got beat the year before, Woody decided that their

defensive line was not in shape. We were going to run the entire game with no huddle. And, really, I think it's the first time where we had hand signals and communication with wideouts. I mean, it's almost like what they're doing today. It was incredible. On the first drive we went right down the field. The first part was that Woody decided we'd run the no-huddle, but we had to be in shape. So, we had to sprint every single day. ...

Zelina: Do you remember how big that defense was? Their smallest guy on the defensive line was like 250, which was huge back then. But Woody thought that with this no-huddle, they'd get tired, they'd get tired, they'd get tired. But ...

Long: I think it set a different tone.

Foley: The whole stadium was astounded. It was like silence, almost. Even though we were moving the ball, and everything was

This 14-yard touchdown run by backup quarterback Bill Long (24) against No. 1-rated Purdue is one of the most storied in Ohio State history.

wide-open and different, the crowd was just, like, watching us as if to say, "Is this really Ohio State football?"

Marsh: Who the heck are these guys?

Polaski: This was a game that was obviously a high priority for us from the beginning of the season, and because of the defeat the previous year. We were prepared. When they came out in a formation, we knew what Purdue was going to do out of that formation. There was nothing they were gonna do to us that we weren't prepared for. And the play Teddy Provost intercepted a pass on, we just switched ... we knew where the two receivers were going to be. We just gave (Phipps) a bad read. He thought the guy was going to be wide open, and Teddy Provost was all over it. Now, to Teddy's credit, he knew that it was coming and this was an easy pass to drop ...

Zelina: That's the toughest catch to make ...

Polaski: Yeah. This was the easy pass to drop. Teddy wrapped it up. If he had a better

arm, he could have cleared the south end zone stands.

Zelina: Didn't Holtz come up with a scheme?

Tatum: He came up with a thing they called "The Robber." It was a game between me and Teddy Provost. When I called "Robber" I would take the deep curl zone and Teddy would shoot up and take the short zone. Ordinarily, it was the other way. I guess the best thing that happened was early in the game we had a regular defense called and I went out and got my hands on a pass in the short flat and almost intercepted it. The next time they came that way we called "Robber" and I guess Phipps read me and just flung it out there and Teddy walked in with it.

Zelina: We were well prepared.

Marsh: That's the first game where I remember all this stuff in the locker room, with Leroy Keyes, Mike Phipps and all that ...

Polaski: Leroy Keyes and Phipps' jerseys were 23 and 15, and they were on the ground.

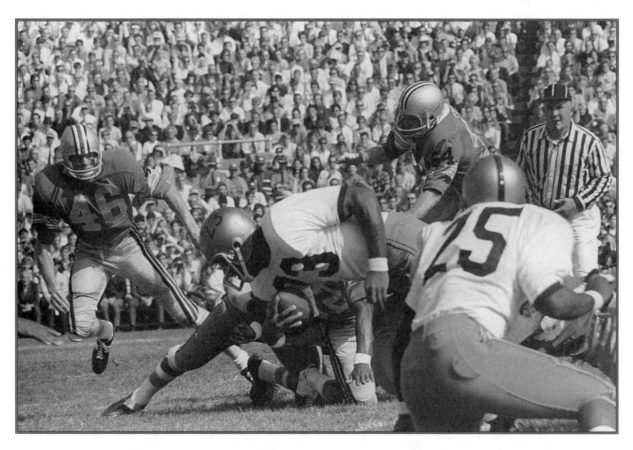

Defensive back Ted Provost (46), closing in here against Leroy Keyes (23), and Jack Tatum were central to the Robber coverage that would allow Provost to intercept a Mike Phipps pass and return it for a touchdown.

And when you walked out to practice, you could walk on it, step on it, spit on it, do whatever you wanted to it. They were two people we were not going to let beat us. And, we didn't "talk" to them.

Zelina: We weren't a talking team.

Polaski: Yeah. To this day, I can remember telling Jerry Levias in the SMU game, "Nice catch."

Nick Roman: Hmmmmm.

Polaski: It was! Believe me. I was all over his little butt and he still caught it. There wasn't any talking. The other guy was allowed to be a good athlete. They were allowed to make plays. Our job was to make sure they didn't, and in this game they sure didn't!

Nick Roman: What the Old Man always told us was that if we were taunted, point up to the scoreboard.

Zelina: It was an unbelievable, hard-hitting game. The score indicated that, and we only scored one touchdown offensively. And I'll tell you, that guy that just walked out of here *(Foley had excused himself)*, he had, every game, this ugly scar on his nose. And he hit so hard he had blood just running down his face.

Marsh: All the time.

Zelina: And I remember Duke and Rufus and Muhlbach. And Muhlbach was blocking a 250-pound guy at 195 pounds, and just, and just, well, it was a war. It was a war!

Worden: We were a better team than they were.

Polaski: That game was a defining moment and it made us a better team. They were No. 1 and averaging 40 points a ball game coming to us, and we shut them out.

Long: Did you know that before that game we weren't selling out the stadium?

Marsh: I'll tell you, Purdue was a cocky team.

Nick Roman: They were.

Center John Muhlbach (53), moving out against Purdue, spent much of the game blocking players fifty pounds heavier than he was.

Worden: They were confident.

Zelina: I could see it in pre-game (warm-ups), they were starting to strut.

Nick Roman: I was hurt and did not get a chance to play against the suckers! But the next year, I did. I was having fun that day. I did the talking that day.

Marsh: You've got a way with words, Nick.

Long: To shut out this team was impossible. Nearly impossible.

Tatum: There was a handful of unsung heroes on that defensive unit. Schmidlin, Nielsen, Urbanik. They were solid. Like I said, once we cut off the sweep, they had a pretty good fullback. And a lot of times they set up Keyes on the outside and would try to pop that fullback up the middle. They just shut off everything up the middle and they forced Purdue to try to run outside and they just couldn't. Those guys were just rock-solid. They were there all the time. ... I'll tell you another guy, my favorite guy, Dave Whitfield. He made me an All-American. He played wide side with me. He took all the blocking out and all I had to do was make the tackle. It was funny, you know, because they would pull two guards and send a back out and he'd take all three out and I'd make the tackle.

If something happened and the back got out on me, we'd go back to the huddle and I'd bitch at him: "C'mon, Whit, you let the back get out on me." He was great, he was great.

Polaski: The crowd enthusiasm came back that day, too. It was one of those days I can remember the crowd in Ohio Stadium.

Nick Roman: They took the goal posts down.

Worden: Yeah, that was something.

Polaski: Most of the time, once the game started, you didn't hear anything when you were on the field. There was an electricity that was there that day ...

Long: I was at the 1970 Michigan game, the 1977 Oklahoma game ... I've never seen a crowd like the one for this game.

Strickland: And then 84,000 people moved down to High Street! It was one freaking party, man!

Nick Roman: I thought they were going to beat us.

Long: I thought they were going to score against us.

Worden: The thing I remember, I was looking at Woody—I was on the sideline—and he caught me eye, and I said, "We got 'em, Coach."

Nick Roman: Our coaches were something! The stuff that happened in the (1997) Penn State game wouldn't have happened on our teams. No way. Those guys were twelve-up and started celebrating, and then Penn State comes back and kicks their butts. You would never see us smiling ...

Brad Nielsen (77) pressures Purdue's offense. He was credited by teammate Jack Tatum with being one of the unsung heroes of the 13-0 upset victory.

Polaski: No. 1 ...

Nick Roman: When somebody was down and we had our foot on their throat, we pushed harder on it.

Zelina: Especially after Billy's touchdown, it wasn't a letdown; it became more intense at that point. It may not have been our biggest victory, but it was our most important.

Polaski: When you start talking about celebrating and all that stuff, when you came off the field you had a spot you were supposed to be. Offensively, they had seats. Defensively, they had seats. If you weren't there, somebody wanted to know why. If information was going to be passed on, you had to be there—not up celebrating when the game's still going on! If your (position) coach wanted to come to you and talk to you, your butt had better be there. There wasn't any celebrating on the sideline back then, because when you came back to the sideline, you came back to be coached again.

Zelina: As I remember, in the fourth quarter of this game, they had a couple of drives down to our 20-yard line ... (Mike) Radtke had a sack and Wagon (Jim Stillwagon) made the interception. ... They moved down there and it was scary in the fourth quarter.

Polaski: They were never out of the ball game, especially with our kicking game. Two scores, and they win.

Long: Coaches today talk about how you can't win without a good kicking game. It's so true. We just managed to do enough other things right.

Zelina: I was an integral part of that awful

kicking game!

Worden: Our coaching staff was really into that football game, more than any other game. (Defensive coordinator) Lou McCullough was just in tears after the game.

Marsh: It was that way all year.

Zelina: We didn't blow anybody, except Michigan, away.

Nick Roman: We were a better team in 1969 and we lost to those guys. In 1968, we were finding ourselves.

(Ted Provost enters the room.)

Zelina: The Tree! The Tree Man!

Nick Roman: We were just talking about you. Where the heck have you been?

Provost: Coaching a basketball game.

Marsh: We were talking about Purdue in 1968.

Nick Roman: He kicked their fannies all by himself.

Provost: It didn't start with that game. It started the year before, when they beat us 41-6. You guys (sophomores) weren't there. We were there. ...

Zelina: We were up in the stadium.

Provost: Ski and I were there. We got humiliated in the secondary. They wiped us out. They could have scored sixty points if they wanted to. We started from there. Woody got us primed for this game starting back then. The electricity was unbelievable for this game. I drove my car down to campus for this game and ...

Zelina: Left it there?

Provost: I left it there. The next day I said, "Where's my car?"

Zelina: Ski was talking about the play you scored on. Do you remember that?

Provost: Yeah. We were covering two underneath, and we would switch it off. I think the play before I had covered the inside guy and Jack (Tatum) had the outside guy. Phipps

With the ball unclaimed after OSU blocked Purdue's punt, Mike Polaski (15) moves in to take charge.

read the play. He saw Jack covering the inside guy and he thought I was covering deep, but I was playing up. It was a no-brainer.

Long: Of all people, Ted Provost, the quietest guy on the team, did the only real celebrating during the game. He throws the ball in the stands.

Marsh: Otie (Jim Otis) copied him one game ...

Zelina: The Michigan game ...

Marsh: Just to prove he had as good of an arm.

Long: No one did that. No one ever did that.

Zelina: And you didn't even get hollered at for that, did you?

Provost: No. No, Holtz told us, "If we score on defense, you guys can do it." *(He turns to Polaski:)* I think you did it on the blocked punt, right?

Zelina: He spiked it!

Polaski: I did spike it.

Zelina: You defensive backs were hot dogs back there.

Provost: Hey!

Polaski: We had to take it when we had the opportunity.

Provost: We had a lot of change-ups, and that was ninety percent of it right there.

Zelina: Keyes was never the same after that ball game. Never the same. Phipps was never the same after that ball game, either.

Otis: Do you remember, Larry, Woody al-

ways used to stand behind us when we were on offense and, you know, he seemed to spend a lot of time with the backs? One of those individual deals. That's all he did.

Zelina: He was the backfield coach, man. ... We moved the ball but we had some penalties and turnovers in that game. We shot ourselves in the foot a couple of times.

Otis: I do remember us having some penalties. We did run the ball effectively against them. And we needed the big plays against them. We needed the big play from Provost. And then the big play from Billy Long ...

Zelina: That really was the springboard to our season. It gave us an indication of what we could do.

Otis: There's no question, and the fact that we made mistakes in the first three games and got away with it. From that point on, when you beat the No. 1 team in the country ... Do you remember the date of that game?

Zelina: Yeah, I'll never forget it. Only reason why was because it was my mom's birthday. It was October 12.

Otis: It was Columbus Day. Do you remember Woody made a speech to us about Columbus? Before the game he gave us a big talk about how Columbus discovered America. And I'm sure the juniors and seniors are taking it all in and the sophomores are looking at each other. But at halftime it might have been a little bit more

Purdue quarterback Mike Phipps (15) backpedals against the Buckeyes. Some players said they believe he never regained his vaunted form after the OSU defense pounded him relentlessly.

meaningful. He said, "They're No. 1 and we're killing ourselves but we're beating them." And how all these kids across America would give their right arms just to be sitting in this room right now where we were. And we went out in the second half and have those two big plays that we talked about, but we took them apart in the second half. I don't remember how Purdue did the rest of the season.

Zelina: I know that Mike Phipps was never the same and Leroy Keyes was never the same after that game.

Smith: What I remember is that Woody did a masterful job at halftime, and it wasn't really him (talking). He brought in Lew Walt to the locker room ...

Nick Roman: He was the commandant of the (U.S. Marine) Corps, a four-star general.

Smith: The commandant of the Marine Corps was in our locker room at halftime! And I'll never forget him standing up and talking about or relating war in the trenches in Vietnam to playing ball and the challenge ahead of us that day. I had gotten word that a friend was killed in Vietnam about two or three weeks before that, a high school friend. And (Walt) was there and there wasn't a dry eye in the locker room. I mean, we could have beaten the Green Bay Packers that day, I think, based on the motivation level. Woody was masterful in the way he planned that, and he knew the young and emotional talent he had on this team and how high we could get.

Pollitt: The other thing about that game, well actually before that game, was we'd get taped down at the stadium. Normally there wasn't much of a crowd (at that time of day) or noise at all when you're getting taped. This game, when we were getting taped, it was loud outside, and it had to be an hour before game time. ... That game you kind of realized in the back of your mind, Hey, this is a different deal. It was rockin' out there.

Jim Roman: When we went out for pregame (warm-ups) at 12:10, they were all over the place already.

White: Most definitely. It certainly was different from the other two games.

Sensibaugh: Whoa!

Nick Roman: In Ohio Stadium, (players) could stand up on the second floor of the locker room and see everything, and we were all going, "Man, this is happening. This is big." We could look down at all the people coming in from the Polo Fields.

Sensibaugh: It was a whole different atmosphere.

Nick Roman: You could hear them!

Polaski: The crowd was up for it, because the No. 1 team in the country was coming in.

Sensibaugh: After this win, whether you read the stuff or believed the stuff they said about us, it was something else! We had just upset, basically ...

Jim Roman: Shut them out!

Sensibaugh: We had just shut out the No. 1 team.

Nick Roman: That was a serious buttkicking!

Sensibaugh: And we started to talk, "Maybe we do have something here, you know?"

Polaski: But even after this game, it happened all the way through the season ... Teams come out now from the beginning of the year wanting to attain the national championship.

Pollitt: It wasn't something we set out to do. It was something that happened to us because of what we did. ... Am I correct on this? Leroy Keyes, on a punt, was the slot man then. And as I remember, there was a play set up where the middle guard and the end man were to hit Keyes and stand him up and Tatum had a 10-yard run and was gonna drill him.

Smith: They take him out and say he had an equipment problem.

Sensibaugh: He goes out, the sub comes in and gets drilled and that was the last time Keyes plays slot man on the punt.

Nick Roman: We were gonna take a shot at him, I remember that.

Polaski: We weren't real worried about returns ...

Marsh: Lou McCullough didn't care about whether you took a cheap shot.

Nick Roman: It was win at all costs.

Marsh: Lou McCullough said he wanted Keyes out, no matter what.

Zelina: When I think about it, we played against some great football players that season.

Otis: Oh, we did!

Sensibaugh: The response of everybody

this week was just so sharp ...

Tatum: At that point, though, I think we were still trying to figure out how good we were. We didn't have a clue at that point. I don't think we knew until the season was over. And that was probably good.

Smith: Does anybody remember McCullough's pre-game

prayer when Woody let him do it? *(Imitates McCullough's southern accent:)* "De-ah Low-ud, please help us to dee-stroy ow-uh en-ih-mee. Thank you very much."

Pollitt: Keep cool, baby, and run those fat tackles to death!

Saftey Mike Sensibaugh (3), handling the punting against Purdue, said the whole team responded well to preparations for the game.

OSU vs Purdue

SCORING

Purdue	0	0	0	0	— 0
Ohio State	0	0	0	13	—13

OSU — Provost, 34-yard interception return (kick failed).
OSU — Long, 14-yard run (Roman kick).
Attendance — 84,834

TEAM STATISTICS

	PUR	OSU
First downs	16	22
Rushing	35-57	67-333
Passing	2-34-129-2	8-16-78-0
Total yards	186	411
Punts-avg.	6-36	4-31.2
Punt returns	1-6	3-17
Kickoff returns	3-5	1-13
Int. returns	0-0	2-35
Fumbles-lost	2-0	3-2
Penalties-yards	4-43	8-96

50¢

OHIO STATE

NORTHWESTERN

HOMECOMING SATURDAY, OCTOBER 19, 1968

CHAPTER SEVEN
Ohio State 45, Northwestern 21

t certainly didn't seem as if those were the No. 2-rated Buckeyes playing their fourth consecutive game at home. At least not at the end of the first quarter, when Northwestern University was clinging to a 7-6 lead. It was the first time the Buckeyes had trailed this season.

Still, an impressive and concussive fourth quarter by the OSU offense left the Wildcats reeling and their coach, Alex Agase, promising to vote the Buckeyes No. 1 in the next poll.

Quarterback Rex Kern nearly was a one-man wrecking crew, totaling 291 yards of offense as the Buckeyes rolled to a 565-yard output. Kern's Northwestern counterpart, Dave Shelbourne, a backup playing in place of the injured Dana Woodring, peppered the OSU defense for 176 yards through the air, and the defense was tagged with the unpleasant distinction of allowing three touchdowns in a game for the first time this season.

"All those accolades, spoken and written (in the wake of OSU's upset of Purdue the week

When you upset the No.1-rated team in the country, you should expect the television cameras to come calling the next week. Such is the case against Northwestern, and the student card section welcomes the ABC-TV Sports crew to Ohio Stadium.

before), made a difference in our defense. (It) softened them up a little," Buckeyes coach Woody Hayes said. "But after (the Wildcats') second touchdown, the defense went to work."

Fullback Jim Otis jump-started the offense with just less than three minutes to go in the first half, snapping a 14-14 tie on a 6-yard run. They would not trail again, although Northwestern didn't exactly roll over. Now Ohio State was beginning to understand what it meant to be the hunted.

"... For two and a half quarters, they moved the ball against us better than anyone," Hayes aid. "We did not especially wear them down, but our offensive yardage was very efficient today where it had not been before. We hammered at the offense all week; they'd heard those nice things, too."

If his Buckeyes were the hunted, they also had to be the haunted, especially where the kicking game was concerned.

That aspect of the Buckeyes' special teams was anything but special. Jim Roman managed just one conversion in six attempts. So concerned was Hayes that he resorted to trickery to make up for the shortfall. After Kern's 7-yard dash to paydirt in the second quarter, Hayes opted for a two-point conversion attempt. Larry Zelina tossed a perfect halfback option pass to backup quarterback Bill Long to push the Buckeyes to a 21-14 lead.

"It's silly," Hayes said of the shortfall of extra points. "It's all in their minds. We're not asking them to kick the ball a mile."

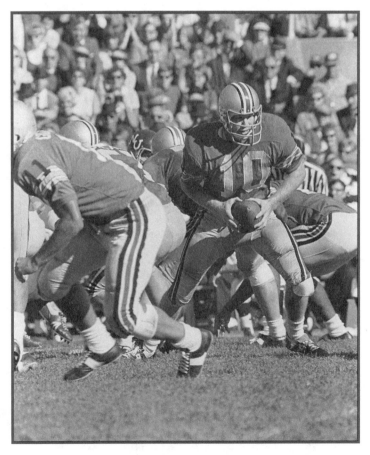

Running room against Northwestern isn't a problem for quarterback Rex Kern (10) and the rest of the offense.

Kern's penchant for finding running room doomed the Wildcats, Agase said. "The guy who hurt us most in the first half was Kern. When he had his receivers covered, he took off and picked up valuable yardage. Their attack was pretty balanced," he said.

Indeed, Kern rambled for 121 of the Buckeyes' 347 yards on the ground. Buckeye passers totaled 218 yards.

Still, in the second half the Wildcats kept coming even after going down 27-14 on Kern's 23-yard scoring pass to split end Bruce Jankowski. They managed to claw their way to a 27-21 deficit before the roof fell in.

The fourth quarter was a work of art for the Buckeyes and their Homecoming faithful. Otis pounded one in on a 6-yard run; sophomore Leo Hayden, seeing extended playing time in place of the injured John Brockington, put up another "six" with a 3-yard run and totaled 51 yards on just six carries; and substitute quarterback Ron Maciejowski hooked up with backup halfback Ed Bender for the closing score on a 37-yard pass.

Said Agase: "We did as good of a job today as we've done against a good football team. We were in the ball game quite a while and had a chance to win. We scored three times, and that's the most we've scored all year ... and against a defense I have a lot of respect for."

If it pointed out anything, this game showed the Buckeyes that nothing would come easy in a title hunt. Next up: a trip to Champaign to face the University of

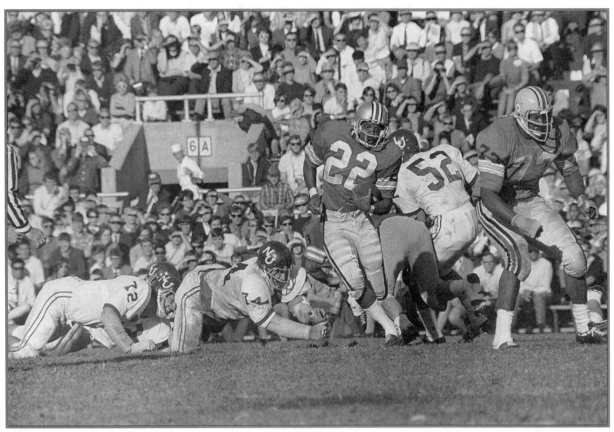

Running back Leo Hayden (22) looks for paydirt against Northwestern. He finished with 51 yards on just six carries and had a 3-yard touchdown run.

Illinois.

Said Hayes: "I am not unmindful that they have beaten us two in a row, and you may quote me."

The post-game huddle

Zelina: We were so hot, even though Northwestern wasn't highly ranked at that time, but it just seemed like we were really ready to play that game, too. They scored twenty-one points on us ...

Polaski: Yeah. This was the 45-21 game?

Zelina: 45-21. Offensively we were going okay. Jan got in and scored in this game.

Polaski: This was the Northwestern team that had that pretty good center, Jack Rudnay. They were a decent football team. They weren't chopped liver or anything like that.

Sensibaugh: One of the guys on the defense came off, and he had grass stains all over his uniform, turf chunks hanging on his helmet. It was Vic Stottlemyer. He came off going,

"I don't know about you guys, but there is one bad *hombre* out there and it's Rudnay."

Polaski: I remember he was hurt at some point in the game and he's pounding the ground. I remember thinking, It's better he's pounding the ground than Vic Stottlemyer's head.

Jim Roman: I didn't start all year, but I played three or three and a half quarters this game, because John (Muhlbach) was banged up. Don't you remember? He had a bad ankle and they had it all taped up ... all the way to his butt! I think (after the Purdue game) we were a little banged up.

Zelina: I think what we're starting to see at this point of the season is the entire offense being used. It's Jan, it's Bruce, it's Brock early and Otie. But I don't think—it was still early—that the coaching staff knew what it had, so they were playing with it. ... They were still having fun with the offense. Everybody was getting involved. And defensively, too, everybody's making big plays.

Middle guard Vic Stottlemyer (69) and teammates make sure this Wildcat is sealed off against forward progress.

Pollitt: If you take that program from "three yards" to what you're seeing here (on a video), this is light years from two to three years previous to this.

White: When I was in high school, I was a wide receiver. What happened here was, Dick (Kuhn) got hurt during practice one day and they moved me inside to the tight end position and I "complained" a little bit about it, but it fell on deaf ears. So, I just thought I was going to be in there for a couple series until he got well and I would move back out to wide receiver. It just never happened.

Polaski: What was it Holtz used to tell us in meetings? "People get hurt playing this game, but knock on wood *(three taps on the table)*, we don't want to see anybody get hurt. People are going to get hurt during the course of this season, and when they do we're just going to have to close ranks and march on—because they're not going to cancel any of our games. We're going to have to continue to play." And that's what we did. The good news was, we had people who could step in and play,

so it never really cost us anything.

Smith: We went three deep at every position. Every position. Northwestern could see that, too.

White: But I don't think we knew that going into the season. That's the thing, I think, as the season progressed ...

Polaski: No, it's just guys got an opportunity to play because something happened to somebody. Some guys came in and did the job.

Tatum: I think they gave us more trouble early in the game than we expected. They scored on us first and they had a few big plays on us defensively that surprised us.

Zelina: We scored a bunch of points and that's when our offense started to really open up. Jan catches a 70-yard TD pass, Jankowski turns the Jet pass into a long TD. Every game somebody else was stepping up. I look at the SMU game, Cowboy (Doug Adams) has an interception, Debevc has a tackle for a safety, Brungard scores three times. The Oregon game Polaski blocks a punt and takes it in for a score, Debevc has an interception, Jankowski catches a long TD pass ...

Tatum: That's what we were talking about; it was always a new guy stepping up. We didn't depend on the same guy every week. It was amazing. Whoever we needed to do it stepped up. ... The only thing I remember about the Northwestern week is we started to get into the Michigan syndrome, because we spent a little bit of time on Michigan that week. A couple days on Michigan and I'm thinking, We're playing Northwestern this week!

Jim Roman: We were starting to play with a little more confidence after these games.

Sensibaugh: Or you get ahead a little bit and you give someone a blow, and all of a sudden they're fighting back.

White: What I recall was a lot of great camaraderie. Guys were saying good things to one another, regardless of whether this person was playing the same position. ... I just recall people saying good things and just being supportive of one another. That's the kind of team we had all season long. That was one of the catalysts that allowed us to be as good as we were.

Kern: Everybody was happy.

Polaski: I'm going to take this to the next season. This thing lasted for two years, and during the course of those years we won twenty-three straight football games. And I can't remember ever saying, "We're so 'bad' we can't be beat." We didn't think that way. We felt amongst ourselves on the field that we were gonna win, but we didn't talk about it or talk that way. You just went out, you had fun and you enjoyed playing whoever you were playing. Winning was the object; that's why they keep score. And that's what we played for, to win. Our coaches did a great job of preparing us, putting us on the field and putting us in positions where we could win.

Nick Roman: But we didn't want to hear that stuff on Hump Day (Wednesdays). It was more, "Just put us in, let us kick some tail and get this over with." That's what this game was about, too.

Kern: Woody would always reinforce that, too,

with the illustration of "that sure-footed mountain goat, who kept one foot in front of the other and stayed focused and continued to work hard every day at the 'fundamentals.'"

Nick Roman: That's right. I was very fortunate to play for two great coaches in Woody and Paul Brown with the Bengals. The first thing we did in Cincinnati was learn how to tackle and learn how to block. Both of those coaches made us start right where you're supposed to start. About three years ago, I did some volunteer coaching at an inner city school ... and the guy says, "Well, tell me what you know about the game." And I said, "Do they still block and tackle?" And he goes, "Yeah." And I said, "That's where it all starts."

Kern: Yeah, you're talking about fundamentals ... look at our play, 26. Mace and I, in our quarterback meetings, used to have so many funny situations with Woody. "Z," I don't know if you remember this one play—it was a Samson. This was kind of a quarterback draw, but at the last second you dumped it off to the tight end ...

White: It was scary ...

Kern: ... You'd just swing it over the middle. So we run this play three hundred times in practice, and you know you're not gonna use it in the game. So

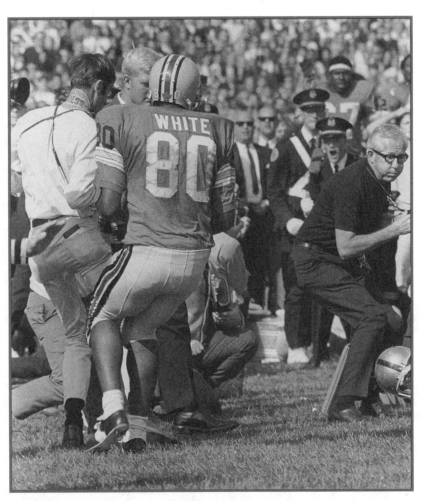

Having the speed to work the sideline, tight end Jan White (80) enjoys a productive afternoon against Northwestern. He scored on a 70-yard pass reception.

we're sitting down in our quarterback meeting. Woody says, "Okay, Rex, you've got first-and-10. What do you call? Second-and five, what do you call?" And Samson was one of those plays for when it was third-and-45. And so Woody's gonna spring the secret-play question on me, and he goes, "Okay, Rex, you're third-and-30 on your own 20. Which play do you call?" I drew a blank. Mace is snickering. And I said, "I'd call Robust 26." Woody says, "Great call. We'd catch 'em back on their heels. Great call! Great call! You call that play anytime. Those linebackers will be frozen, we'll give the ball to Otis! Great call."

OSU vs Northwestern

SCORING

Northwestern	7	7	7	0	—21
Ohio State	6	15	6	18	—45

OSU — White, 72-yard pass from Kern (kick failed).

NW — Herrington, 15-yard pass from Shelbourne (Emmerich kick).

OSU — Kern, 7-yard run (Long pass from Zelina).

NW — Shelbourne, 4-yard run (Emmerich kick).

OSU — Otis, 6-yard run (Roman kick).

OSU — Jankowski, 23-yard pass from Kern (kick failed).

NW — Hittman, 7-yard pass from Shelbourne (Emmerich kick).

OSU — Otis, 6-yard run (kick failed).

OSU — Hayden, 3-yard run (kick failed).

OSU — Bender , 37-yard pass from Maciejowski (kick failed).

Attendance — 84,834

TEAM STATISTICS

	NU	OSU
First downs	18	28
Rushing	44-104	69-347
Passing	16-31-184-2	10-19-218-0
Total yards	288	565
Punts-avg.	7-44.6	4-38
Punt returns	1-0	3-20
Kickoff returns	7-115	3-45
Int. returns	0-0	2-0
Fumbles-lost	4-0	3-0
Penalties-yards	4-40	8-78

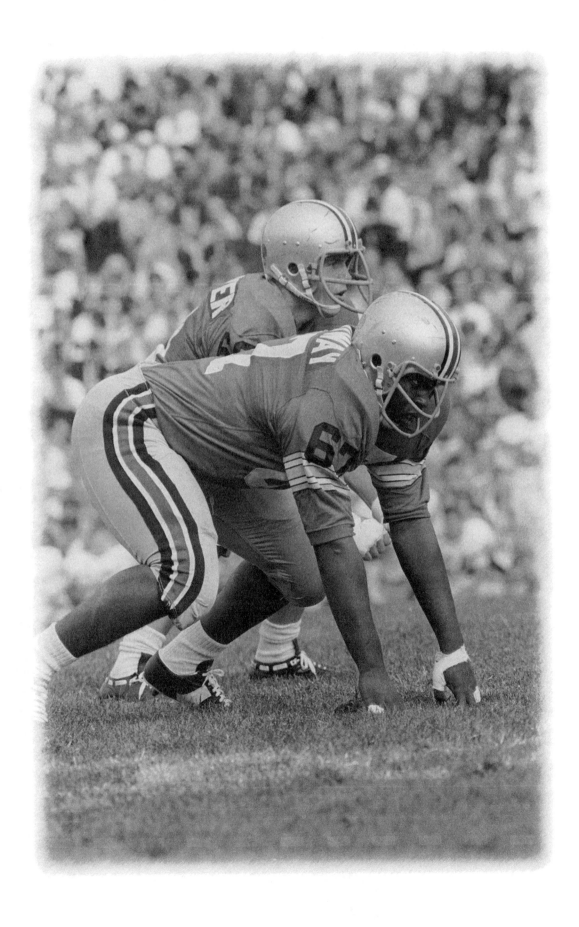

ILLINOIS
OHIO STATE
58th Annual Homecoming

Saturday, Oct. 26, 1968
Kickoff 1:30 P.M.

PROGRAM
50c
MAGAZINE

CHAPTER EIGHT
Ohio State 31,
Illinois 24

With just four minutes, thirty-eight seconds to go in the game, No. 2-rated Ohio State and its Big Ten and national title hopes were sagging against the ropes. The Buckeyes had given up twenty-four consecutive second-half points against the host Illini and were staring at the possible end of their eight-game winning streak over two seasons. It was 24-all, and stomachs in every corner of Buckeye Kingdom were churning like the wheels of a semi rig mired in three feet of mud.

Enter Ron Maciejowski. Because feisty sophomore starting quarterback Rex Kern had to leave yet another game with yet another injury, this one to his head, coach Woody Hayes opted for Mace, the Super Sub, as a result of his running ability.

"We were on our own 30," Hayes said, "and I felt we'd probably have to run ourselves out of trouble."

Seer, he.

With second-and-16 at OSU's 30-yard line, the sophomore Maciejowski calmly engineered the game-winning drive, which was capped by fullback Jim Otis' 2-yard run. Along the way, he passed to wingback Larry Zelina for 10 yards, ran for 12, nailed a pass to Zelina on the 27 (which the speed demon ran to the 4), then turned things over to Otis, who, with two 2-yard bursts, saved the season with 1:30 left.

"Zelina had a doggone good day, and Maciejowski, too," said Hayes, the master of the understatement.

The 24-0 halftime lead was nothing more than a memory after backup fullback Ken Bargo barged in from the 2-yard line and ran in the two-point conversion for the apparent tie.

In that productive first half, the Buckeyes held Illinois to 84 yards and three first downs while rolling up 294 yards and 17 firsts. So where did OSU go after halftime?

As the second half began to unfold, Zelina's reception from Kern accounted for a yard. Then Kern was picked off, giving rise to Illinois' first scoring drive, this one of 30 yards. The Buckeyes' defense began to give up big chunks of yardage to Illini fullbacks. Something was missing. More to the point, some bodies were missing: linebacker Dirk Worden, cornerback Tim Anderson, safety Mike Polaski and defensive end Mark Debevc, starters all, were out with injuries.

So, the Illini went on the offensive once more, churning up turf and Buckeye defenders—and converting two fourth-down plays along the way—to score again. Ohio State helped Illinois climb to dead-even with a personal foul penalty deep into another Illini drive. A series of short gains from the 10-yard line was culminated by Bargo's 2-yard TD dash and a third two-point conversion.

Michael Radtke
No. 55 — Linebacker

James Roman
No. 52—Center

Arthur Burton
No. 21—Linebacker

And then Maciejowski saved the day.

Kern finished 12-of-21 for 102 yards with two interceptions, Maciejowski was 2-of-2 for 54 yards, Leo Hayden ran 14 times for 77 yards, Kern 14 for 57 yards, Otis 11 for 72 and Zelina eight for 61. Zelina led the receivers with five catches for 76 yards. And Jim Roman made all four extra-point attempts and a 21-yard field goal.

"It was good for us to play a game like that," Hayes said.

If he only knew.

The post-game huddle

Zelina: What about those splits, Schmids, did you notice that?

Schmidlin: Oh, you could feel it, yeah. It took a while to decide what to do. Did we get on the phone ...

Stillwagon: No, it was just fingertips. If we could go like this *(demonstrates)* and touch each other's fingertips. We didn't care what splits they had. We'd just go like this *(demonstrates again)* and if we could touch each others' fingertips they would take that feeling of spreading us out and run that big fullback right up in there. We started keeping ourselves at arm's length, we started shutting them down. That's what turned it around for us.

Schmidlin: I remember one interception, I don't know if you (Stillwagon) hit it or who hit it, but the ball went straight up in the air. I was standing there underneath it, waiting for it

Gary Roush
No. 59—Tackle

Bruce Smith
No. 17—Defensive halfback

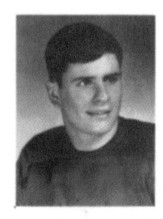

James Gentile
No. 39—Linebacker

Edwin Bender
No. 19—Halfback

John Sobolewski
No. 91—End

William Hackett
No. 51—Middle Guard

to come down. And it was coming into my arms, when all of a sudden Brad Nielsen comes FLYING out of the other side, and he's grabbing and he's scraping at that sucker and I'm trying to pull it down. I pulled it in and said, "If we keep this up, we're gonna lose." I grabbed that sucker and shoved it into his gut, and he took off. He got the Buckeye leaf for that ...

Zelina: And Schmids was saying, "Aw, shucks."

Schmidlin: Yeah, I was.

Zelina: I think they fed off that, because we (had) scored twenty-four straight, real fast points and then we didn't score again. I mean they stopped us in the entire third and fourth quarters. And ...

Polaski: That's because you guys didn't get the ball very much in the second half, because ...

Zelina: They were running it.

Polaski: They were just eating up the clock, and they just kept moving the chains. They were moving the ball three and four yards down the field, and they just kept moving the football.

Stillwagon: They had a big fullback.

Schmidlin: A big one.

Tatum: I don't remember too much about the first half because I didn't play the first half.

Zelina: Why's that?

Tatum: I had sprained my ankle against Northwestern and they held me out as a pre-

David Cheney
No.75—Tacle

Jim Oppermann
No. 76—Tackle

Richard Troha
No. 71—Tackle

Robert P. Smith
No. 87—End

Kevin Rusnak
No. 23—Quarterback

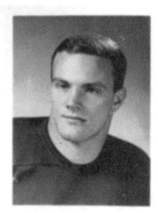

Randy Hart
No. 65—Guard

cautionary measure. And during the second half, Illinois started moving the ball against us, scored two TDs. Woody told McCullough to put me in. McCullough says, "I can't put him in, Coach. He's not taped up and he's got a twisted ankle and can barely run." So they were a TD down and they finally score to tie the game up. Woody comes up to me and says, "Get taped." So I got taped and went in.

Stillwagon: I remember Bill Mallory comes to me at halftime (with OSU up, 24-0), and he says to me, "We're going to play Vic (Stottlemyer)." And I said, "Great." I'd taken my tape job off and I was listening to that halftime speech about Abraham Lincoln campaigning

on the riverbanks over here, and I'm going, "Holy cow!" We didn't talk about football. We talked about Abraham Lincoln. I remember thinking, Man, that's really great. I can take my tape job off. And then later in the game when things got screwed up, I said, "I don't have a tape job." This was a wild game wasn't it?

Zelina: It was scary. And I don't know whether there was a (second-half) letdown, because that was the first game we got off to a real big lead, and maybe offensively we might've …

Jim Roman: I think we might've gotten a little complacent.

Polaski: But, again, it might have been the

Larry Qualls
No. 58—Center

Vincent Suber
No. 37—Linebacker

Ralph Holloway
No. 67—Guard

Ray Gillian
No. 11— Halfback

Leophus Hayden
No. 22—Halfback

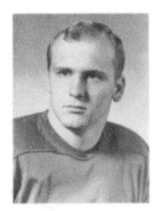

Larry Zelina
No. 16—Halfback

best thing for us, because if there'd been a blowout there it might've led to big-headedness down the road. As it was, Mace had to come in and win it at the end ...

Zelina: Yeah, we snapped their garter ... But we could do no wrong in the first half.

Otis: You know, sometimes when that happens, sometimes you let up a little bit. First of all they come out in the second half and score three TDs against us. And they run for the extra points and make them all. And tied the game. Then Kern gets hurt and Mace comes in and he throws a big pass to you.

Zelina: Then we bang in there a couple times and you finally score to put us ahead.

The thing was, though, we almost scored with too much time on the clock. When we went ahead, there was still a little over two minutes left, we kick off and they start moving the ball again.

Otis: Do you think we passed a little too soon?

Zelina: Finally, Baugh intercepted a pass with a little less than a minute left and we won the game.

Otis: We were lucky to get out of that game.

Polaski: And all of a sudden, it's back to reality. Everybody you play is gonna be good. You've gotta play for the full sixty minutes.

Jim Stillwagon
No. 68—Middle Guard

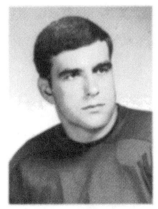

Brad Nielsen
No. 77—Tackle

Jan White
No. 80—End

OSU vs Illinois

SCORING

Ohio State	3	21	0	7	—31
Illinois	0	0	16	8	—24

OSU — Roman, 21-yard field goal.
OSU — Otis, 1-yard run (Roman kick).
OSU — Kern, 1 1-yard run (Roman kick).
OSU — Kern, 16-yard run (Roman kick).
ILL — Johnson, 2-yard run (Johnson run).
ILL — Naponic, 2-yard run (Naponic run).
ILL — Bar go, 2-yard run (Bar go run).
OSU — Otis, 2-yard run (Roman kick).
Attendance — 56,174

TEAM STATISTICS

	OSU	IL
First downs	25	21
Rushing	55-290	51-200
Passing	14-23-163-2	9-23-102-3
Total yards	453	302
Punts-avg.	4-32.2	6-43.2
Punt returns	0-0	6-77
Kickoff returns	3-39	0-0
Int. returns	3-36	2-26
Fumbles-lost	3-0	0-0
Penalties-yards	3-29	5-45

James Conroy
No. 95—Center

Jim Coburn
No. 47—Halfback

Steven Crapser
No. 94—Defensive Tackle

Daniel Aston
No. 86—End

Jack Marsh
No. 49—End

Ted Kurz
No. 64—Guard

50¢

Parents' Day

MICHIGAN STATE

OHIO STATE

Saturday
November 2, 1968

CHAPTER NINE
Ohio State 25, Michigan State 20

t took defensive end Dave Whitfield's second fumble recovery of the fourth quarter to ensure the Run for the Roses would not end face-first on a brick wall.

As Michigan State quarterback Bill Triplett was looking for a receiver, Whitfield's running mate at defensive end, Mark Debevc, came barreling in to crush the Spartans' passer and force the fumble.

Remaining true to their "We're Just Keeping Things Interesting" script, the Buckeyes stormed out to a 19-7 halftime lead only to have the visitors close to within five points at 19-14.

Coach Woody Hayes' game plan had the Spartans reeling in the first half. Hayes eschewed his normal strategy, preferring to script the plays and again have the offense run what the Buffalo Bills would popularize in the 1980s, the No-Huddle Offense. He also ordered passing plays on—could it be?—first down.

"We have been running on first down, and they knew it," Hayes said. "We also believed their defense against running was better than their pass defense, and still I believe it was."

Before Whitfield would put the fire out, quarterback Ron Maciejowski, coming in for Rex Kern, who was sent to the bench with a horrible ankle sprain, took command once more to help OSU keep Pasadena in its sights.

Mace, who had logged just twenty minutes of previous game experience, still managed to chalk up another game-clinching scoring drive; he capped it by calling his own number for a 2-yard run into the end zone.

As had been the case in previous weeks, the defense all but saved the day—and possibly the season—for Ohio State. The Buckeye defenders pounced on four Michigan State fumbles and picked off three Spartan passes. In a wild and woolly fourth quarter, OSU brought down MSU ball carriers for losses six times (and totaled 69 yards in losses for the game), and Doug Adams got in on the fumble-recovery party with a key pickup early in the fourth quarter just as MSU had crossed midfield and was threatening to effect a sustained drive.

Over on offense, Maciejowski had help from Larry Zelina (seven carries for 63 yards, two receptions for 48), Leo Hayden (10 carries for 48 yards) and Bruce Jankowski (eight receptions for 88 yards and one TD). Before departing, Kern was 9-of-12 passing for 138 yards and a 14-yard scoring pass to Jankowski.

"Larry Zelina was our best back today," Hayes said. "He made some real big plays for us."

Maciejowski also had help from the bench, his coach said.

"We called most of his plays. It would not

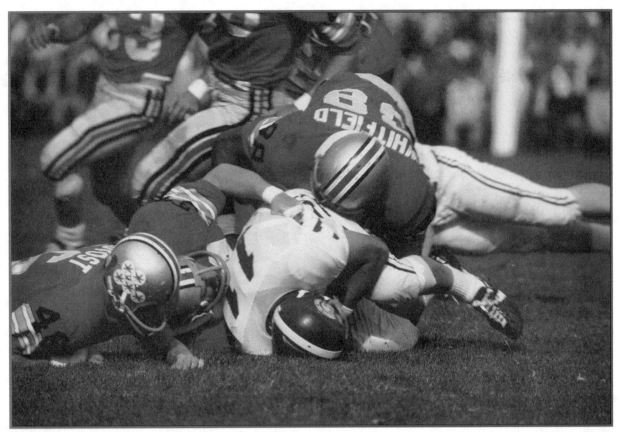

Dave Whitfield (88) makes another statement for the defense against Michigan State. He recovered two fumbles in the fourth quarter.

be fair to him if we didn't," Hayes said. "Kern called all of his plays, usually at the line of scrimmage, although it's difficult with about 85,000 people in the stadium and 75,000 of them are rooting for you."

Still and all, it wasn't until Whitfield made the last of his recoveries that the Buckeyes and their fans could relax. Then, and only then, could they begin to ponder the fact that their team was riding the crest of a ten-game unbeaten string which began the previous fall against, oddly enough, Michigan State at East Lansing with a 21-7 conquest.

"Once again, we beat ourselves," MSU coach Duffy Daugherty said of his team, which the week before had upset Notre Dame, 21-17.

"You can't turn the ball over that often. When you turn the ball over seven times to a team as good as Ohio State, it's a wonder if you don't get beat worse than that."

Hayes said Kern would be held out of the upcoming game at Wisconsin.

Was a quarterback controversy on the horizon?

The post-game huddle

Zelina: That was a tough ball game.

Polaski: You've gotta remember, they were only two years removed from being national champs, and they pounded Notre Dame and had a lot of good players still left from that team.

Sensibaugh: If you check the scores, the week before Michigan State had really beaten Notre Dame. Everybody (the rest of the season) we played was coming off big wins. Michigan State was. Then Iowa; (Ed) Podolak had set a record the week before he played us with over three hundred yards. It seemed like everybody was coming off a huge game when they got to us. (Michigan's Ron) Johnson had a huge game (347 yards) before they played us.

Otis: What I remember about this game, they came out and played a pretty bold game against us. They came with virtually an eleven-man line against us which didn't do any good for me, obviously. And they had just beaten Notre Dame the week before. So they were sky high and I remember this was another turning point for us because we would have to rely on more than just the running game to be successful. And it seemed like they were going to start using you a little bit more. So with them jamming the line of scrimmage they had to give up something, and they're going to give up the passing. That is, if we can get someone off the line of scrimmage. ... And I was a little disappointed in myself this game.

Zelina: Well, there wasn't much you could do about it. They jammed it up.

Otis: Yeah, they jammed it up, but you caught a couple big passes and Bruce Jankowski made some real big catches, one of them made the cover of *Sports Illustrated*. And Rex got hurt again and Mace came in and saved the game for us again with his leadership.

Zelina: As I recall, they had a man in every gap and dared us to run.

Otis: See, that's when the QBs can start putting it in and then try to get outside. You probably ran the reverse in that game, didn't you?

Zelina: Yeah, we ran a couple inside reverses and then we ran the 58 and 59 where we faked the dive to you and I came around from the wingback position and we'd option on the outside. The ground game wasn't real effective that day. When Woody finally decided to throw the ball, it did help us.

Otis: Woody had a tendency of being pretty stubborn about trying something other than the running game.

Zelina: Oh, you think so? ... Wagon, you guys got ready for Triplett, because he was the

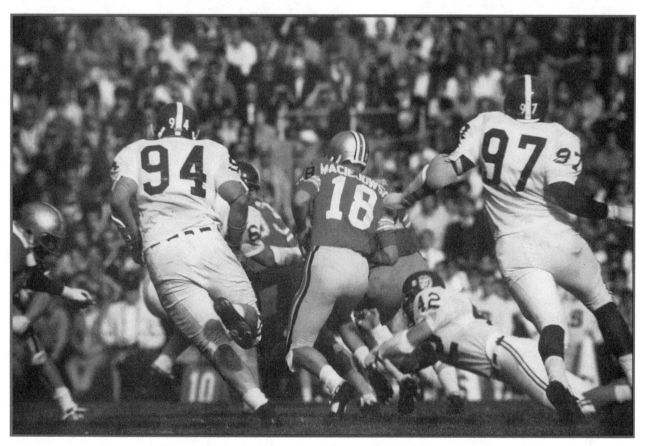

Quarterback Ron Maciejowski (18) finds a seam against the Spartans.

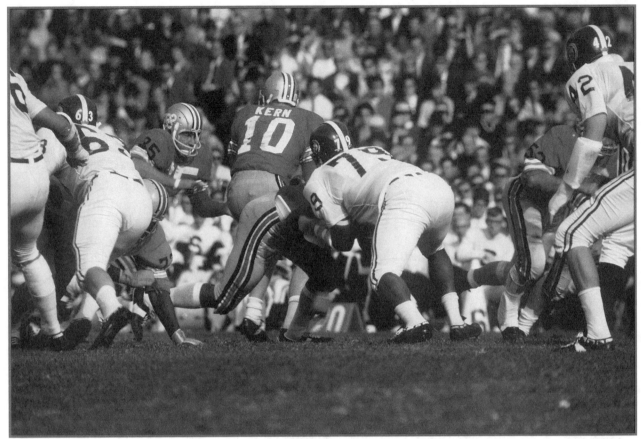

Rex Kern (10), a fine running quarterback, takes MSU's "dare" to run.

option quarterback. Do you guys (on defense) remember doing anything special for Michigan State?

Stillwagon: I remember Debevc and Whitfield were supposed to tackle Triplett. ... *(Points to Zelina:)* Didn't you knock Saul out of that game?

Zelina: That was the next year, our junior year.

Stillwagon: Because I'm playing against his brother—they had a really big team, didn't they? ...

Zelina: Yeah. No. You're right. It was that game, because we were running the option and I came back and I cracked on his brother ...

Stillwagon: He was a linebacker ...

Nick Roman: One was a linebacker and the other was a guard or something ...

Stillwagon: Rich and Ron.

Zelina: You're right. I tore his knee up on that. I didn't mean to. I just threw ...

Nick Roman: You threw low in practice, too, you SOB.

Zelina: Our junior year, one punt I caught

and his brother just came down and nailed me. He got up and he said, "The name is Saul." ...

Stillwagon: And you said, "Oh, sorry, I didn't mean to hurt your brother." ...

Zelina: So the next punt is the one I took back seventy-three yards for a touchdown, and I said, "The name is freakin' Zelina." ... They were a tough team, though (in 1968). They had a tailback by the name of Love that was a heck of a running back.

Stillwagon: The only thing I remember about Michigan State was that (MSU coach) Duffy Daugherty came down before the game ... and he says, "How're you doing, Jim?" And Woody comes over, and he says (to Daugherty), "What the heck are you doing down here? (Then, to Stillwagon:) "Don't listen to this guy! He's just trying to soften you up. (Then, to Daugherty:) "You get back up that field or I'm gonna kick your butt!"

Tatum: They had a couple big plays over the middle and they scored on us, but I remember we kind of wore them down and the defensive line played a good game that day. They were harassing Triplett and I remember he got so nervous one time because we had been blitzing him that he took a snap and the ball went straight up in the air and I think Debevc recovered it. I think he was just getting worn out from the blitzes we were throwing at him and he saw it coming and tried to pull away from the center too quick and the ball just went straight up in the air.

Zelina: Michigan State was a good team.

Tatum: Yeah, they had some horses.

Zelina: I think another thing we saw here (on the video tape) was the versatility of the offense, because Jankoswki had a big game this game with his receptions. And on defense, too, it seems as if everybody's getting interceptions. Rads (Mike Radtke) had a big game. Radtke had a lot of big plays.

Nick Roman: (Debevc) was hurt. Rads was *Sports Illustrated's* player of the week. He had, like, four sacks and an interception. ... You guys were playing them, and I was operated on October 28.

Donovan: They were all bigger than me.

Zelina: I will say that we probably had the finest set of pulling guards in the Big Ten with (Tom) Backhus and (Alan) Jack and Phil (Strickland) and Brian. It was ...

Stillwagon: They were quick.

Zelina: It was phenomenal. They were 205, 207, 210 (pounds), but they could all run. They could ALL run. Can't run now, can we Brian?

Donovan: Not much.

Zelina: We pulled against Michigan State, and it was awesome. Just awesome.

Schmidlin: In talking about the guards, I was at Buffalo (of the American Football League) and they needed somebody to run offensive guard (in practice). I went in and did several plays, and at that point the coach just shook his head and said, "It must have been nice to be Ohio State." Just because I was doing the job well enough. He wondered how I got on defense when I was doing that well on offense.

(The players instantly begin imitating a dump truck shifting gears, sort of like the noises Schmidlin purportedly made when he played.)

OSU vs Michigan State

SCORING

Michigan State	0	7	13	0	—20
Ohio State	7	12	6	0	—25

OSU — Otis, 1-yard run (Roman kick).
OSU — Jankowski, 14-yard pass from Kern (kick failed).
MSU — Triplett, 1-yard run (Boyce kick).
OSU — Otis, 3-yard run (pass failed).
MSU — Foreman, 13-yard pass from Triplett (Boyce kick).
OSU — Maciejowski, 2-yard run (pass failed).
MSU — Love, 1-yard run (pass failed).
Attendance — 84,859

TEAM STATISTICS

	MSU	OSU
First downs	18	24
Rushing	59-134	54-214
Passing	9-15-137-3	16-26-215-1
Total yards	271	429
Punts-avg.	5-38.6	7-37.2
Punt returns	4-60	3-17
Kickoff returns	5-73	5-58
Int. returns	1-7	3-36
Fumbles-lost	5-4	2-1
Penalties-yards	4-26	7-71

Zelina: There's that old truck again! ... Ski, remember anything about that interception?

Polaski: Just that I thought Baugh was gonna catch it, and then he didn't ...

Nick Roman: Tip drill!

Polaski: ... Yeah, that was something that we did everyday in practice. Holtz was always out there during it all, telling us, "Boys, I've got a golden arm. I can throw all day.

Nick Roman: He had a golden tongue, too.

Zelina: Isn't he amazing?

Polaski: It was fun.

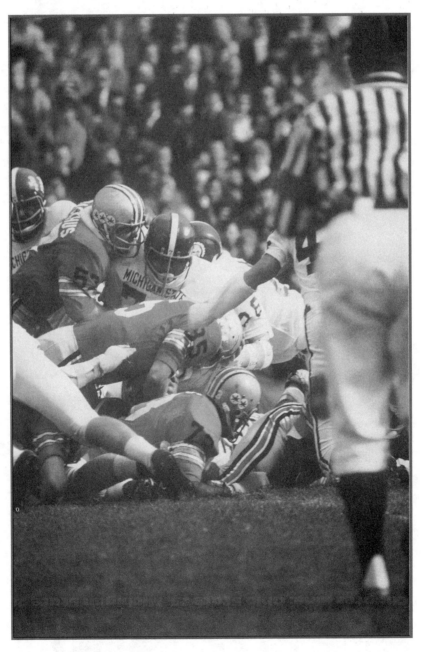

One of the best pulling guards in the Big Ten, Tom Backhus (57) does his level best to move the pile against Michigan State.

Wisconsin
Ohio State

Saturday, November 9, 1968, 1:30 p.m.
Camp Randall Stadium, Madison

CHAPTER TEN
Ohio State 43,
Wisconsin 8

Ron Maciejowski, starting at quarterback for the injured Rex Kern, passed for 153 yards and rushed for an additional 124 as the Buckeyes went full-throttle through the out-classed host Badgers.

Although his statistics wouldn't indicate it, Mace said he was nervous.

"I felt kinda funny, yeah," he said. "I was nervous. I got the bad part out first. The second half is my half, man. Rex can have the first half."

Coach Woody Hayes was pleased with Maciejowski's performance.

"We scored four of the first five times we had the ball," Hayes said. "He has a deceptive little run, hasn't he? He's got a deceptive little cut that fools 'em."

As Maciejowski was racking up the second-best total offense output of the season for the No. 2-rated Buckeyes, wingback Larry Zelina and fullback Jim Otis made the most of their playing time on the artificial surface of Camp Randall Stadium. Zelina pulled in five passes for 120 yards and one touchdowns, while Otis scored on a pair of 2-yard bursts and had 94 yards on 18 carries.

This one, statistically, was as lopsided as the score indicates. OSU had 27 first downs to Wisconsin's eight, and 468 total yards to the 187 for the Badgers.

With Maciejowski running the offense to near perfection and Hayes declaring Kern available for the next game, the coach was asked if Kern might have lost his job to his classmate.

"It's nice to have problems like that," was all Hayes would say.

By now, two more opponents and two hours of football were all that separated Ohio State from its quest for the Rose Bowl.

The post-game huddle

Otis: Mace started that game. It was kind of the Maciejowski-Zelina show in Wisconsin.

Zelina: Yeah, we ran a couple of delay passes that Mace threw to me and we busted for some long gains. And he hit me for a TD pass in the first half. Mace was great that game. He rushed for 120 yards and passed for 150 yards. That's when I started to see what you were talking about.

Otis: That's right. We started doing more.

Zelina: Yes. By this time the opposition was setting up to stop you and the running game and Woody began to use the other guys on the team and we had Jan White making big plays and Jankowski making big plays and every once in awhile I got lucky and made a play or two and Mace was making big plays. Be-

Ron Maciejowski
No. 18—Quarterback

Tom Bartley
No. 33—Linebacker

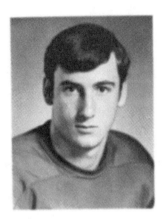

Brian Donovan
No. 66—Offensive Guard

cause until they saw the new offense we had, they were setting up to stop the fullback.

Otis: I'll tell you one thing, one thing about Maciejowski: He didn't have many opportunities to show how good he was but I'll tell you one thing, I'll never forget that game. I mean this guy, he did his thing. He ran, he passed, he did it all.

Zelina: That's it. How many guys on that team could have played anywhere in the country? But you start someone and unless that guy screws up, you don't replace him. I mean you're at fullback and Brockington is waiting, but as long as you gain your yardage and don't fumble, you're going to play. Ray Gillian shared

time with me and Ray was a heckuva athlete. I get hurt and he helps win the Rose Bowl for us. Jan White gets hurt and Dick Kuhn goes in. It was just phenomenal. And I could go on and on.

Otis: That's the thing I think these teams saw in the Michigan State game and the Wisconsin game. We started to do more and they saw more people being involved, and they found out that jamming the run was not the answer to stopping our offense.

Zelina: Hey, that was our first game on artificial turf.

Muhlbach: There were only two teams that had artificial turf, and I think both of them were put in that year ...

Chuck Aldrin
No. 85—End

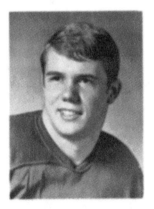

Doug Adams
No. 63—Linebacker

Bruce Jankowski
No. 82—End

Bob Trapuzzano
No. 17—Linebacker

Phil Strickland
No. 62—Guard

William Pollitt
No. 97—Linebacker

Zelina: Yeah, Wisconsin and Michigan State.

Schmidlin: I remember this was a cold, cold day.

Zelina: But that was our easiest game of the year. And I don't remember much, other than it was cold and I …

Polaski: Wisconsin's the only place we played that year that had artificial turf.

Zelina: … I do remember …

Muhlbach: They were not very good.

Nick Roman: We were probably practicing against Michigan that week.

Schmidlin: Who was our graduate assistant from Wisconsin?

Stillwagon: Eric Rice.

Schmidlin: I remember him one time in the locker room saying, "You guys have no idea how hard they prepare for Ohio State."

Nick Roman: What'd he say?

Polaski: Not successfully.

Schmidlin: Not successfully, yeah. No, but with lots of intensity. They wanted very badly to beat us. I think it was part of their downfall, overemphasizing.

(Let's face it, dear reader: This game was a blowout. The players have little to discuss at this point and seem more intent on getting to the Iowa game. This way, please.)

Jack Tatum
No. 32—Halfback

Ted Provost
No. 46—Safety

Tim Anderson
No. 26—Halfback

Mike Sensibaugh
No. 3—Safety

John Muhlbach
No. 53—Center

Charles Hutchinson
No. 72—Tackle

OSU vs Wisconsin

SCORING

Ohio State	10	0	20	13	—43
Wisconsin	0	0	0	8	— 8

OSU — Roman, 28-yard field goal.

OSU—Zelina, 7-yard pass fromMaciejowski (Roman kick).

OSU — Maciejowski, 5-yard run (Roman kick).

OSU — Otis, 2-yard run (Roman kick).

OSU — Otis, 2-yard run (kick failed).

WIS — Ryan, 1-yard run (Voigt pass from Ryan).

OSU — Maciejowski, 1-yard run (kick failed).

OSU — Maciejowski, 10-yard run (Roman kick).

    Attendance — 40,972

TEAM STATISTICS

	OSU	WIS
First downs	27	8
Rushing	61-301	45-88
Passing	15-25-167-1	6-15-99-1
Total yards	468	187
Punts-avg.	3-41.7	9-32.3
Punt returns	4-24	0-0
Kickoff returns	1-28	7-114
Int. returns	1-0	1-5
Fumbles-lost	4-1	3-3
Penalties-yards	4-24	7-76

Paul Huff
No. 34—Fullback

William Urbanik
No. 79—Tackle

Michael Polaski
No. 15—Saftey

John Stowe
No. 92—End

Horatius Greene
No. 44—Halfback

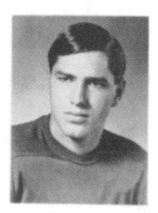

Ed Lapuh
No. 84—End

David Foley
No. 70—Tackle

Dirk WOrden
No. 56—Linebacker

William Long
No. 24—Quarterback

THE COLLEGE GAME

OHIO STATE vs. IOWA

NCAA

MEMBER

OFFICIAL PROGRAM 50 CENTS

NOVEMBER 16, 1968
IOWA STADIUM

Bill Long (24) sets to pass against Purdue as the OSU sideline contingent, including Woody Hayes (black cap), looks on.

Mike Polaski comes up with the ball for the Buckeyes' defense.

Defenses saw a lot of Leo Hayden (22)—but mostly from behind, as Michigan State does here.

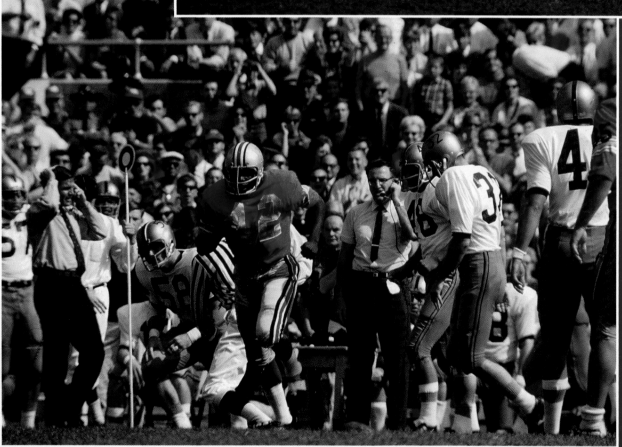

Don't give him an inch, or he'll take a mile. That's what Purdue learned about John Brockington (42) at the end of this play.

Offensive guard Alan Jack (61) gets into position as quarterback Rex Kern (10) prepares to hand off against Northwestern.

Defensive ends Dave Whitfield (88) and Mark Debevc (83) join defensive backs Ted Provost (46) and Mike Sensibaugh (3) and the rest of the defense in the huddle against Michigan.

Is it a run or a pass? Only crafty quarterback Rex Kern (10) knows for certain against Oregon.

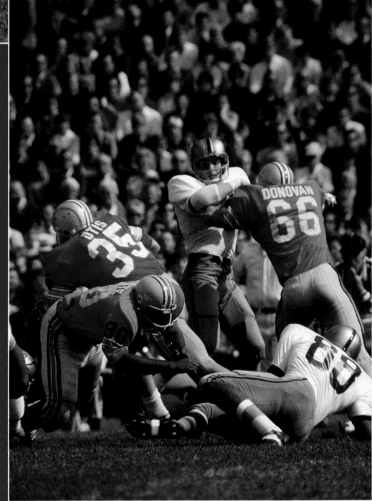

Jan White (80) and Brian Donovan (66) hold off Purdue defenders as Jim Otis (35) pounds through the line.

WE'VE GOT THE GAMES!

SPORTS • RADIO

THE FAN

1460•WBNS

HOME OF THE BUCKEYES

**The Ohio State Buckeyes
Radio Sports Network**

FOLLOW THE OHIO STATE BUCKEYES ON YOUR LOCAL STATION:

Akron WAKR 1590   Archbold WMTR FM 96.1   Ashtabula WFUN-AM 970   Barnesville WBNV-FM 93.5

Bellefontaine WBLL-AM/WPNT-FM 1390/98.3   Bryan WQCT-AM/WBNO-FM 1520/100.9   Bucyrus WQEL-FM/WBCO-AM 92.7/1540

Canton WHBC-AM 1480   Celina WKKI-FM 94.3   Chillicothe WBEX-AM 1490   Cincinnati WBOB-AM 1160

Cleveland WKNR-AM 1220   Columbus WBNS-AM/FM 1460/97.1   Coshocton WTNS-FM/AM 99.3/1560

Dayton WING-AM 1410   Delaware WDLR-AM 1550   Dover/New Philadelphia WJER-FM/AM 101.7/1450

East Liverpool WOHI-AM 1490   Elyria WEOL-AM 930   Findlay WFIN-AM 1330   Fremont WFRO-AM/900/99.1

Gallipolis WJEH-AM 990   Hillsboro WSRW-AM/FM 1590/106.7   Huntington, WV WHRD-AM 1470/WZZW-AM-1600

Ironton WIRO-AM 1230   Jackson WKOV-FM 96.7   Kenton WKTN-FM 95.3   Lancaster WLOH-AM 1320

Lima WIMA-AM 1150   Logan WLGN-FM/WLGN-AM 98.3/1510   Mansfield WMAN-AM 1400   Marietta WMOA-AM 1490

Marion WMRN-AM 1490   Marysville WUCO-AM 1270   McConnellsville WJAW-FM 100.9   Middleport WMPO-AM 1390

Middletown WPFB-AM 910   Millersburg WKLM-FM 95.3   Mt. Vernon WBZW-FM 107.7   Napoleon WNDH-FM 103.1

Newark WCLT-AM 1430   Norwalk WLKR-FM 95.3   Painsville WBKC-AM 1460   Parkersburg, WV WLTP-AM 1450

Paulding WERT-FM 99.7   Portsmout WNXT-AM/WNXT-FM 1260/99.3   Sandusky WLEC-AM 1450   Sidney WMVR-FM 105.5

Uhrichsville WBCT-AM1540   Upper Sandusky WYNT-FM 95.9   Van Wert WERT-AM 1220   Warren WRRO-AM 1440

Waverly WXIZ-FM 100.9   Wheeling, WVA WOMP-AM 1290   Wooster WQKT-FM/WKVX-AM 104.5/960

Youngstown WKBN-AM 570   Zanesville WHIZ-AM/FM 1240/102.5

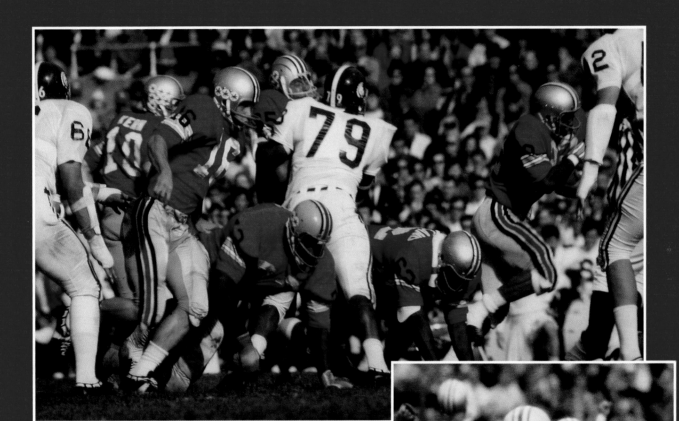

In Ohio State's 25-20 victory over Michigan State, the Buckeyes' Leo Hayden (22) bursts through the line for a long gainer.

Larry Zelina (16) sprints down the Buckeye sideline toward the end zone.

CHAPTER ELEVEN
Ohio State 33, Iowa 27

Book it: Michigan at Ohio State for the Big Ten Conference champion ship and a trip to the Rose Bowl.

OSU rated No. 2 and winning its eighth game of the season and twelfth in a row over two seasons, had its hands full this day.

The host Hawkeyes, even after trailing 19-0, found a way to answer OSU in the second half. They scored twenty-one fourth-quarter points, the last with nine seconds left. OSU pounced on a second-consecutive, on-side kick and ran out the clock.

Finally, it was time to begin thinking about the game with Michigan.

But for this day, the headlines belonged, for the most part to the rushing attack. Out of the Tight-T formation, fullback Jim Otis romped for a career-best 166 yards and two touchdowns.

"Maybe we're not running him enough," Coach Woody Hayes said of the junior bruiser.

Rex Kern went all the way at quarterback, steering the Buckeyes to a slight 420-387 margin in total yards. Support came from halfback John Brockington (10 carries for 62 yards, including a 22-yard touchdown dash) and wingback Larry Zelina (six carries for 50 yards and four receptions for 67 yards).

The OSU defense bottled up Iowa's sensational running back, Ed Podolak, limiting him to 45 yards on 15 carries. But the concerted effort to stop Podolak resulted in the Hawkeyes' quarterbacks having a good day. Larry Lawrence was 13-of-20 for 178 yards and an interception and Mike Cilek was 7-of-11 for 68 yards and an interception.

Iowa coach Ray Nagel was effusive in his praise of Ohio State.

"They're a fine, fine football team," he said.

"There's no doubt about that. Gosh, I'm impressed with (Otis). He's a fine, fine runner. Ohio State is strong on offense and defense, but I would say their greatest strength is on defense."

Said Hayes of the late Iowa scoring barrage: "I would rather be in the position of playing stay-ahead football instead of catch-up football. Given a choice, I would always prefer the former.

"It wasn't easy to stay ahead of an explosive team like Iowa. We had that twelve-point lead at halftime, and in the second half managed to stay *that much* ahead of them ... right up to the end."

And since the final score is all that counts,

The defense rises up, holding Iowa on third down.

there's ample reason to rejoice over the onset of Michigan Week.

The post-game huddle

Stillwagon: I actually remember ...

Zelina: Sullivan?

Stillwagon: Yeah, Tim Sullivan. He got in a motorcycle wreck the next year and they had to take half his foot off. But he was tough ... and they started running up the middle. And who was that guy, Niland? He used to play for Dallas? He was over there. I came out and my face was all bloody, and someone on the sideline said to me, "Oh, my God. You should see your face." I said, "Why?" He said, "It's all bloody. I don't know if I want to get into this stuff!" So Billy (Urbanik) gets in and we take Sullivan— there were two or three of us who took him into the other side—and we were getting up, and he gets up and hits Mark Stier. And Billy goes up to him and says, "Don't you ever hit

my man! I mean it!" and he kicks him in the head. ... That was a heckuva game, wasn't it?

Zelina, Nick Roman *(in unison)*: It sure was.

Jim Roman: They told us not to take our helmets off.

Stillwagon: Oh, yeah, I forgot about that ...

Polaski: Iowa City was one of the worst places we played. ... This was one where they spat on you when you come out of the tunnel. They poured Cokes on you. You were told to put your helmet on when you came out of the locker room. The stairways came down, and they were really steep; you had to worry about getting hurt coming down the steps to get to the field.

Stillwagon: That's when the kid said— when Woody Hayes was giving his (pre-game) speech—and the kid comes in and says, "Wait a minute." Woody says, "What the heck do you want?" And the kid says, "I've gotta tell you one thing. Tell your team to keep their helmets on, because people will drop stuff on them." And (Woody) heard that and went back into his speech. We (the Super Sophs) only played out there one time, didn't we?

Zelina: Yeah, just once.

Muhlbach: You guys remember this? Woody sent the team out. And then Woody came out on the field by himself, because he loved it when they booed him. I could never understand why he wouldn't come out with everybody else—at least to protect himself. But after years of looking back and knowing the way he was, when he came out on the field and everybody was booing, he loved it.

Stillwagon: That's when McCullough says *(going into the southern accent),* "Jest rim-im-ber, bo-ahs. They laid out all week now, and they started packin' the dogs and the girls and the farm stuff so that when they git to the game, ever'body would be here."

Muhlbach: Do you guys remember (equipment manager John) Bozick? This was

HIS team, the Iowa Hawkeyes. He always did something a little special during Iowa week.

Stillwagon: I think every game was Homecoming (in the minds of the opponents). Every game was The Game, and when you got by that then you started all over again. That year, what I remember the most was that there was never a breathing time. We'd win one game ... well we did slip through ...

Zelina: You look at the scores and there was a lot of close games.

Stillwagon: We were in passing gear a lot, so ...

Polaski: And with McCullough being defensive coordinator, it was a deal where no matter what we did the week before we didn't play "well enough, not as well as we should." They always beat into your head (that) there was room for improvement and they always did a great job of selling the next opponent. There was never walking on the field feeling that you were gonna steamroll somebody because we

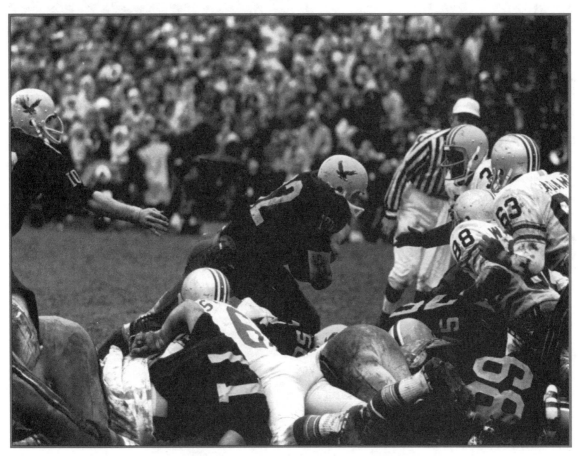

Iowa pounds away, but to no avail, against the OSU defense.

were obviously better than they were, but you felt like you had to play every week and we were always prepared. I'll go back to what Jim said earlier: Whether we liked Lou or not, the man prepared us. We never set foot on the field during that period of time that we weren't prepared for what the other team was gonna show us. They never surprised us by giving us something we hadn't seen. ... *(Getting back to the Iowa game, especially the post-game:)* It was nice to be warm and dry ...

Muhlbach: It was miserable, miserable weather to play a football game in.

Zelina: This was a tough game in bad weather. They scored twenty-seven points.

Tatum: They did that late in the game with passing. They brought in another QB by the name of Larry Lawrence. He came in and was throwing passes all over the place. Got them back in the game. I don't think we were

looking beyond this game. I think we were too keyed up to stop Podolak. And I think once we got him stopped we might have kind of relaxed a little bit. And we weren't prepared to stop the passing game.

Zelina: Do you think we looked past Iowa with Michigan coming up?

Otis: No. You're only looking at the score, because we beat the crap out of Iowa. The only thing that Iowa did was pass at the end of the game. The only place we bent a little bit that game was pass defense. And they made the game closer than it was. I don't know what Podolak had that game, but it wasn't much.

Polaski: Like I said, their fans were downright nasty. I can remember being on the sideline when I was out of the rotation and having somebody actually throw something at me and hit me with it and telling me, "Polaski, 15, YOU! Get down! I paid for these seats and I

Quarterback Rex Kern (10) barks out signals at Iowa.

didn't pay to look at the back of your head." I mean, we were that close to them ...

Zelina: Yeah, that was a terrible place to play.

Polaski: They were just ugly.

Stillwagon: That game was a big game. Podolak had just set the record that stood for many years. After the game ...

Zelina: I don't remember anything from after the game until we got back to practice on Monday (the first official day of Michigan Week.)

OSU vs Iowa

SCORING

Ohio State	6	6	14	7	—33
Iowa	0	0	6	21	—27

OSU — Otis, 7-yard run (kick failed).

OSU— Kern, 3-yard run (pass failed).

OSU — Otis, 1-yard run (Roman kick).

IOWA — Lawrence, 1-yard run (kick failed).

OSU — Kern, 1-yard run (Zelina kick).

IOWA — Podolak, 3-yard run (Melendez kick).

OSU — Brockington, 22-yard run (Roman kick).

IOWA — Manning, 12-yard pass from Lawrence (Melendez kick).

IOWA — Reardon, 9-yard pass from Lawrence (Melendez kick).

Attendance — 44,131

TEAM STATISTICS

	OSU	IOWA
First downs	22	23
Rushing	71-337	45-141
Passing	5-12-83-2	20-32-246-2
Total yards	420	387
Punts-avg.	5-37.8	6-42.3
Punt returns	3-17	2-40
Kickoff returns	5-34	5-49
Int. returns	2-17	2-9
Fumbles-lost	0-0	1-1
Penalty yards	29	45

CHAPTER TWELVE
Ohio State 50, Michigan 14

In his first season as a varsity player, sophomore starting safety Mike Sensibaugh was so driven by all that was at stake for this, the annual showdown with That Team From Up North, that he composed the following hand-written note.

Need it be said? This is probably the biggest week of your life. How can one game have more at stake than Saturday's? The only way the Rose Bowl can live up to its reputation (which hasn't been the best in recent years, because the best teams haven't played) is by having OSU represent the Big Ten.

A game between the No. 1 and No. 2 teams—both undefeated—would be perhaps the greatest college game of "all time."

There is one game between you and that.

When the 85,000 fans watch you playing Saturday, they will be seeing you play at the most famous football school, down through the years, in America.

There have been many big games played here ... many great players ... but none any bigger than Saturday's.

Why? Look at what's at stake:

1. The Big Ten championship.
2. The Rose Bowl trip.
3. OSU's winning streak.

4. The chance of a perfect record while at OSU. And last, but not least:
5. Just the thrill of beating Michigan.

For three hours Saturday you will get an opportunity that everyone thinks about, few get anywhere close to and only one percent of one percent of all college football jocks receive: "Going to Pasadena."

This is a chance to earn more than you could expect in all your OSU playing days.

But the challenge is great, even immense for the best team—and you again are demanded to prove your capabilities—does not always WIN.

Mistakes could be fatal—and never forget that. Remember how bitter defeat is because if you don't you might let up for one second and lose. This will not be an ordinary game, so no matter what occurs, always be psyched, never let your head beat you. You will have enough opposition from the Wolves. Ahead or behind, play with the greatest of your skill, for one minute's break can turn into the next minute's disaster. So don't give them anything extra ... but if you do, and even you, yes you, are human ... try not to let it happen again. Play with the pride you know you have and you've worked so hard to get.

The game of your life is here, so "dream the impossible dream" because it's not out of reach ... for Saturday at 4:30 "there will only be one."

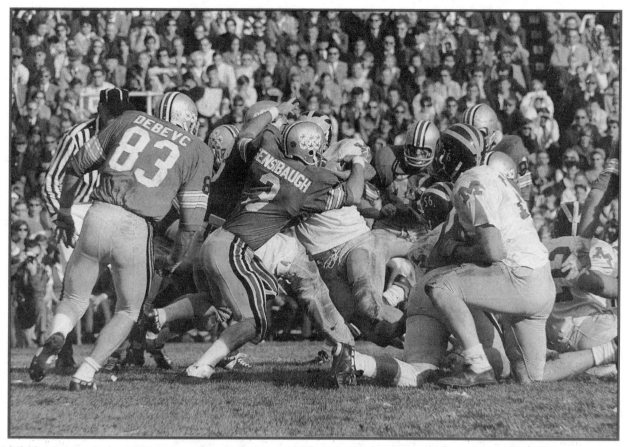

A Michigan player is greeted by the quick tackle of safety Mike Sensibaugh (3) as Mark Debevc (83) closes in for insurance.

THERE IS NO GLORY LIKE VICTORY.

■ ■ ■

Bring on Southern Cal!

With everything on the line, Ohio State fairly took the ball and rammed it down Michigan's collective throat in the second half en route to as convincing a victory as Ohio Stadium had seen in years.

The defense all but contained Wolverines halfback Ron Johnson, who had run for 347 yards the previous week against Wisconsin. He managed 91 yards on 21 carries and scored both Michigan touchdowns.

With rolls of toilet paper streaming down from C Deck seemingly in answer to every big play and the record crowd of 85,371 rocking the Horseshoe, the Buckeyes pounded Michigan's defensive front relentlessly after taking a 21-14

halftime lead. It was about to become "lights out" for That Team From Up North.

After fullback Jim Otis banged in from the 2-yard line to double the difference, this one was all but over. Still, the scoring onslaught continued. Larry Zelina contributed a 6-yard run from wingback, Jim Roman nailed a 32-yard field goal, quarterback Rex Kern scrambled in from the 3-yard line, Otis added another 2-yard burst and then capped the magnificent barrage with a 1-yard score. For those of you counting at home, that's thirty-six unanswered points against the No. 4-rated team in the nation.

Coach Woody Hayes, calling it "the best victory we ever had," admitted after the game that he truly believed his team was a year away. With thirteen sophomores in the starting units, could this have been expected?

"(The sophomores) could have become fatheaded after a win like they had over Purdue, but they didn't do it," Hayes said, adding, "our offense and defense was superb. We stopped a guy who had 347 yards last week. He only had one good run today (a 39-yarder to set up one of his two 1-yard TD runs). It was a heck of a football game, I thought.

" ... All our kids played real good football. What has happened before was that the offense would have a good day and the defense would stutter around some. Then, another game, it would be the other way around.

"We said that if they ever put it together, both played well the same day, we would have something. This was it."

With tackles Rufus Mayes and Dave Foley clearing the way, it was a runner's paradise on the Ohio Stadium turf. Otis led the way with 143 yards on 34 carries, the bootlegging Kern 96 on 19, Zelina 92 on eight and Ray Gillian 66 on five as OSU piled up 421 yards and 24 first downs on rushing plays.

The OSU coaching staff wanted the Buck- eyes to run the ball, because, as Hayes said, "We are all pragmatists and always go for the hole in the fence."

The defense, while perhaps not as perfect as it was in the victory against Purdue, earned additional stripes with its effort. Cornerback Jack Tatum and linebackers Doug Adams and Art Burton each had an interception, and Mark Debevc recovered a fumble, to choke away any hopes Michigan had of an upset. Michigan quarterback Dennis Brown, despite his three interceptions, managed a 14-of-24 outing for 171 yards, but did little if any damage. He was hounded constantly by the swarming Buckeye defense; he carried the ball 10 times for minus-6 yards.

Hayes, who said after the game he wanted to score fifty points, actually put Otis back in the game to do the honors. "He said, 'I can get it for you' when we were bogged down going for the last touchdown," Hayes said. "We did want to get fifty points ... not exactly running the score up, but I don't feel comfortable these days without fifty points. Teams are so explosive on offense anymore. It's unbelievable how they can come back."

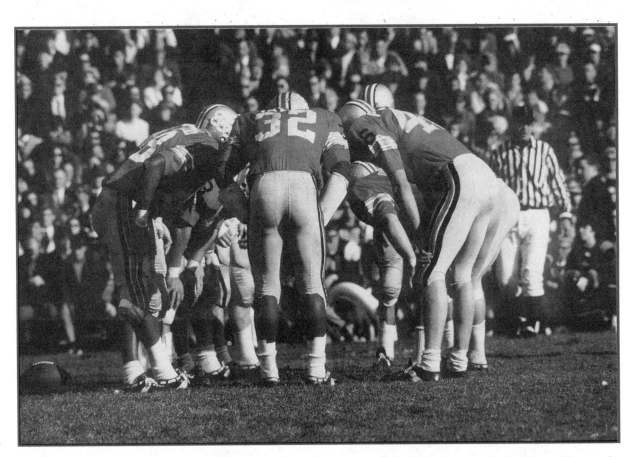

The defense huddles in anticipation of another Michigan play and eventually kicks the door to Pasadena wide open in the 50-14 blowout.

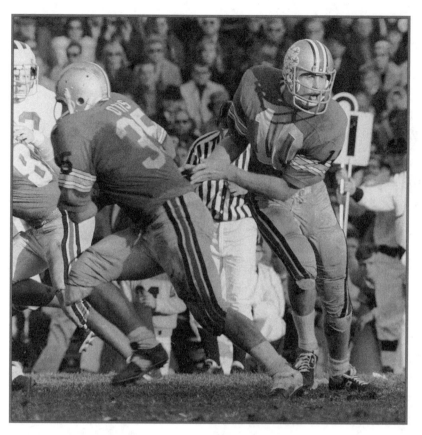

Fullback Jim Otis (35), plowing into the Michigan defense, had a game-high 143 yards and four touchdown runs.

After Otis' final touchdown, his sixteenth of the season which broke by one the record set in 1955 by Hopalong Cassady, Hayes elected to go for two points. When questioned about it after the game, he said center John Muhlbach was hurt and kicker Jim Roman had to play center. Other accounts have Hayes responding to the question of why he went for two points thusly: "Because the SOBs wouldn't let me go for three!"

Michigan coach Bump Elliott took no exception to the try for two.

"I didn't think he poured it on," he said. "In a ball game like that, he's playing to win. No, I don't think he poured it on."

Elliott expected the Wolverines to face a challenge from the Buckeyes' defense, but it was the offense that had him talking. "Take a look at their offensive line and you've got to respect them. They're awfully strong," he said.

This monumental victory was punctuated by fans swarming the field and ripping down the goal posts — "I didn't think they'd ever get them out of there," Hayes said — for an im-

promptu parade down High Street to the State Capitol. After nearly eight hours of constant partying, Hayes showed up with Columbus Mayor Jack Sensenbrenner at the Statehouse. It was midnight. The band was there. The cheerleaders were there. Six thousand fans, among them some celebrating Columbus police officers, refused to let the celebration end.

Said Hayes: "That really was a great victory, wasn't it?"

"There's only one thing bigger than this," said Zelina, "and that's the Rose Bowl."

Goodnight, O.J.

The post-game huddle

Foley: In the Michigan game, uh ...

Nick Roman: Woody put you and Rufus side by side ...

Foley: Woody comes up with this unbalanced line for the Michigan game, with Rufus Mayes and myself side by side. Jan White's a heckuva blocker and we got this strong-side attack, and I'm telling you we're knocking Michigan off the ball! ... We knew we could kick their butts, and let me tell you that second half was the butt-kicking of all time. It was like true Ohio State football. ... If you go back to innovation, the things that we did that year were completely different than football was nationally. Defensively and offensively. I don't think Woody got enough credit for the innovation that year. It really was a complete turnaround.

Polaski: That year, we were not three yards and a cloud of dust.

Strickland: No, we weren't.

Polaski: Jankowski caught thirty-something passes ...

Strickland *(deepening his voice):* Three things can happen when you throw the freaking ball ...

Long: I know it ... . If you had played on the line in 1966 and then played on the line in 1968, you'd have felt the difference.

Foley: The game plan was different and the personnel was different, too ...

Strickland: I'll tell you what was different about the personnel! I came from an all-black high school in Cincinnati, and when I got to Ohio State, I had never seen so many white people *(Strickland makes his eyebrows dance.)* ... in one place. Really, I think we had more blacks on a scholarship basis than ever before at that time.

Tatum: Well, for me it was probably different than for anyone else on the team. I had strep throat all week and didn't practice a day. I wasn't even sure I was going to play. Got better Friday and played Saturday.

Zelina: Hey, you pulled a Zelina, didn't you?

Tatum: Let me tell you something else funny. Every year we played Michigan, the two years we beat them I had strep throat. I still had my tonsils and I'd get sick every fall. I didn't get to practice all week but that was the first time, since I was from Jersey, I wasn't really into the big game, you know, the Michigan-Ohio thing as much as some of the other guys who grew up knowing about it. That's the first time I got a sense of how big the game was. Because The Woods took us out of the dorms during the week. There were, like, thousands of students running around our dorm and he came and put us in a hotel to get away from all the hoopla.

Zelina: What a game, and that's one of those where you did something, Tate, that wasn't supposed to be possible. Remember?

Tatum: Oh, yeah,

on Ron Johnson. He said that he had never been caught from behind. On this play, I shot the gap on a blitz and Johnson split me and Whitfield, he went inside of us. I was in Michigan's backfield and I was scared because I thought I had screwed up so I thought I'd better go get him.

Zelina: Well, that play was one of your trademarks, Jack, and that was the spark for us.

Tatum: Well, that's what we were talking about before. Me and Whit had talked about it, and we both felt like there was no way anyone was supposed to run that side of the field. And when (Johnson) broke through there, we felt like we had let down because that was our territory—and you're not supposed to run it.

Zelina: You were the kind of player that was as quick as you had to be to make the play—and that was a gift.

Tatum: By this time of the season I was just happy to make plays because people

It's not all straight-ahead running for the Buckeyes against Michigan as guard Phil Strickland (62) leads halfback John Brockington on a keeper.

started to run away, and toward the end of the season I was only making a couple of tackles a game. I started feeling like a twelfth man out there sometimes.

Zelina: Johnson had a huge game the week before he played us. I remember it being intense.

Polaski: When we went into the game, we were No. 1 and they were No. 4. So obviously you're looking at two real good teams that were going to be matched up. And if they beat us, they're going to jump way up in the polls. And they had Ron Johnson who was being touted in the same breath as Leroy Keyes and O.J. Simpson as being the great running backs in the country that year. So this game had a lot of potential ... the Big Ten championship, a trip to the Rose Bowl and a high national ranking.

Zelina: It was unexpected. I remember I was numb after the game. I just couldn't believe what had just happened. I couldn't believe it happened.

Nick Roman: It was a tight game for awhile.

Zelina: But as far as it being as perfect a game as we could possibly play ... I just think everything went right for us that game. I don't think we were thirty-six points better than they were.

Smith: We sure were with the coaches.

Stillwagon: To me it was just another game. I didn't know Michigan from friggin' Iowa. It wasn't that kind of game for me. I was amazed by how people celebrated. I thought Purdue was a bigger game, you know, than that game would ever be. No offense, but I didn't really know Michigan-Ohio State was that big of a rivalry. ... I think our team was really groomed. In those years, that was the reward, to win. I mean, our team was so beat to snot from practice that you liked playing the game. I think the Purdue game was more hyped, though, than this game. The Rose Bowl and Purdue were really bigger.

Muhlbach: I remember when we were juniors and we played up at Michigan. Heck, there were only fifty-thousand people in the stands. ... You know, I always thought that

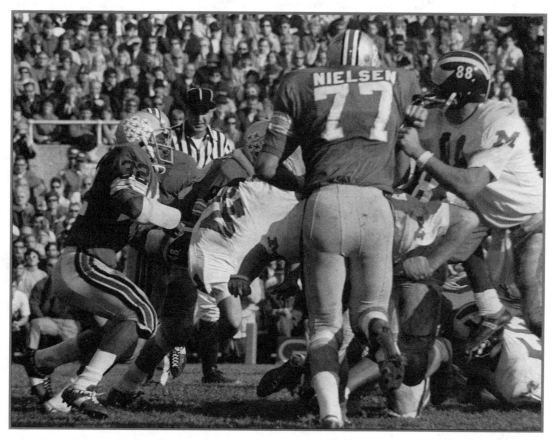

Never is a long time, as Michigan running back Ron Johnson can tell you. Saying before the game that he never had been caught from behind, Jack Tatum (32) changes all that by dragging Johnson to the Ohio Stadium turf.

Michigan State, for some reason—and maybe it stems from our sophomore year when they were so highly rated, and those guys were like gods—and we darn near beat 'em back then. They were more about a better kind of rivalry; the kind of game you really had to get yourself pumped up for.

Nick Roman: Michigan had had losing seasons for a couple years.

Muhlbach: It's amazing how when you're not in the sport, or you're not participating or you're outside, how the media just builds this hype up.

Nick Roman: I've been very lucky ... that we came up in an environment where we had a rivalry, Massillon, McKinley, and we knew what big games were about and how people on the outside reacted to them. I can't tell you how fortunate I really was to be able to come here and play Michigan. And then to play for Paul Brown (at Cincinnati) when they played Cleveland, and Pittsburgh, too. But that didn't even come close to McKinley or Michigan.

Polaski: I don't remember how much the press even talked to us, but (we weren't) nearly as accessible as kids are today.

Nick Roman: Heh-heh-heh.

Jim Roman: We were just happy to be there and having fun.

Nick Roman: We didn't need the media. ... The Old Man used to say, "Let the scoreboard do your talking." And that's what we did.

Zelina: Yeah. We ran the 28 and 29 and the counter-8 and counter-9. I remember it because it was the first time all year I got to carry the ball. What we'd do is run the 28 and 29 to the strong side of the unbalanced line, and we ran the counter to the short side and had Brian and (Tom) Backhus and the other guards ... remember you pulled to the weak side? And that's what we were busting them with.

Polaski: The ones you were busting up the sidelines?

Zelina: Yes.

Nick Roman: Did their defense react to it?

Donovan: They didn't know what to do the first time we came out with it. Then, when they shifted over to adjust, that's when we came back with the counter to the short side.

Zelina: That was the key to what we did

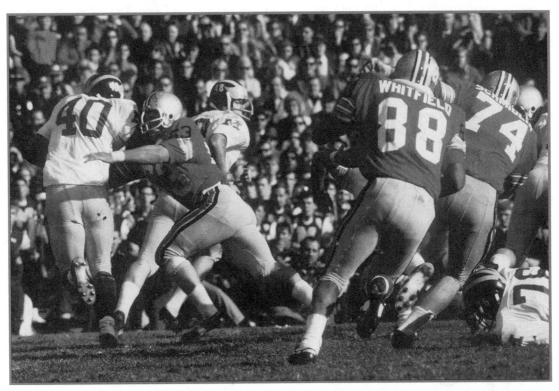

Paul Schmidlin (74) and Dave Whitfield (88) collapse Michigan's front wall as Ron Johnson is brought down again.

offensively. Do you guys remember on the defensive side of the ball what you did to prepare?

Polaski: The only thing that I remember was we were going to feature the Fire game. We were coming from the wide side with Whitfield and Tate trying to collapse that side of the line of scrimmage because we didn't want them to run that ...

Stillwagon: Sprint draw.

Polaski: Yeah, the sprint draw with Ron Johnson.

Nick Roman: On the short side, we'd bring the short-side end and have the linebacker move outside. We'd have a short-side Fire game, but we had the linebacker there to contain them.

Polaski: We were looking for penetration. What we didn't want was for them to get the ball five to seven yards deep behind the line of scrimmage and start looking for holes. We wanted to make the decision for them.

Zelina: Was the secondary in man-to-man (coverage) that game or zone, or was it that combination that you had?

Polaski: That all depended on the down and distance and formation. Whatever they showed us, whatever the down and distance was, we were programmed for whatever we thought they were going to give us out of that set, and we'd call the coverage accordingly. Then if they came out of the huddle and lined up in a formation that dictated a change, then we would make a change call.

Zelina: What was McCullough like that week, do you remember?

Polaski: You couldn't have put Vaseline on a needle and gotten it up his butt!

Bartley: The shelf in his locker was nothing but Maalox ...

Stillwagon: I remember coming back from the movie (Friday, the night before the game) and the bus was real dark and you couldn't see anything and Lou said *(imitating McCullough),* "Hey, Andy, they's more press pay-ses, they's fahty-five more press pay-ses fah thee-us game; they a-gonna be watchin' thee-us game in Brah-zeel! Thee-us is gone be the bee-gest game they ev-uh was!" Man, I can still hear that.

Zelina: Schmids, how about your emo-

tions? How did you feel?

Schmidlin: I've been thinking about that. Looking at the whole thing, there was a regular pattern of preparation for every game in the sense that on Sunday you went in and watched film and after the film you got some additional information about the team. And then you'd be ready for your test on—what?—Thursday before the team meeting. And I'm amazed. I don't remember ever reading the paper other than the results of our game, but as far as worrying about anyone else, the focus was on do the fundamentals and playing the game. For me personally, I know I had my best games against Michigan. At least I thought I did.

Zelina: You're from Toledo?

Schmidlin: And because of being from Toledo, I would hear it all summer long about Michigan. I spent my summers there ...

Stillwagon: You shouldn't have stayed that long!

Zelina: I kind of felt one of the unique things about the team was that the coaches, I mean they'd work really hard to get us up for the game. But the problem I've had with some of current OSU coach John Cooper's teams is that everybody says, "Well, he didn't have the boys ready." But I think in a game like the Michigan game if you're not ready to play, you shouldn't be on the field. I think the coaches had to be careful to make sure that we weren't ready to play too soon.

Jim Roman: Remember Woody used to say you can't make a fist too tight? You start clenching your fist, you get fatigued. You have to stay loose.

Zelina: That's why I was curious how McCullough was. Because if the coaches get too tight, it can transfer to the team. Woody seemed to be under control that week.

Schmidlin: Looking at the films from the previous year, that's one thing I remember for the Michigan game. I kind of remember shaking my head, just kind of saying, "You've learned a lot since last year, haven't you?"

Polaski: I always liked Lou McCullough, because I always thought he was funny. Now he did a lot of mean, crazy things sometimes but that was probably more motivational than anything. He would get started on me, and he hadn't been north of the Mason-Dixon Line for thirty-five years, you know, and he'd get started with that sarcastic drawl.

Zelina: Brian Boy, do you remember anything about getting ready that week? What was Earle like?

Donovan: He was kind of rah-rah. "C'mon, c'mon, we can do it!" He was nervous. I remember he came and saw me sitting in class one day.

Zelina: He was just making sure you were in class!

Donovan: He told me, "This is a big game. We've got this opportunity, we'll never have this opportunity again." You know, from the standpoint that it was to everyone's benefit. It would be a feather in the coaches' hats as well as the players'. You know, if we could pull this off ... But he was extremely nervous about it, but he never screamed or hollered about it. He was more motivating than anything.

Zelina: Did you guys go to Earle's that week?

Donovan: Yeah, I think we did.

Polaski: We did it all year long. All the defensive backs went to Holtz's house. On Thursday nights, we all went to his house. It wasn't any big deal. We had pop and chips and sat around and talked. I will say this: He prepared us. We played hard, and he wanted us to play well and he wanted us to win. But he always made it fun. We never went to practice and didn't have fun. We busted our butts. There was no way with his triple-butt (drill). But sometime during that practice we always ended up laughing.

Zelina: What's the triple-butt?

Polaski: It was a tackling drill that Holtz had. You had two sets of pylons set ten yards apart. And you'd start a ball carrier and a tackler. The ball carrier's going half-go and the tackler's going half-go the first butt. When he says, "Go," the ball carrier runs standing up, offering his numbers. The tackler comes up and form fits; butt's supposed to be down, your back's supposed to be straight, your head's supposed to be in the numbers. You shoot your

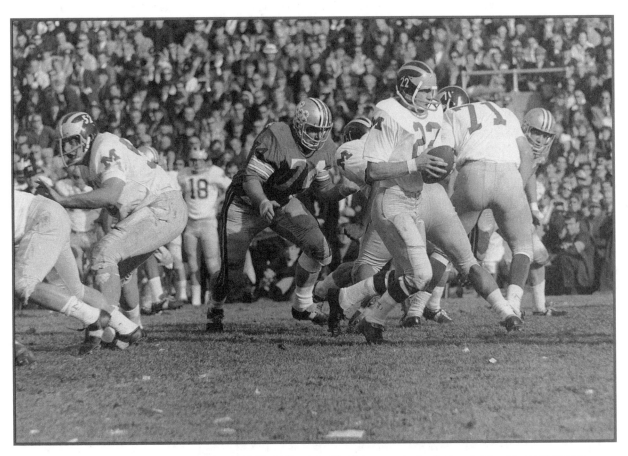

Focusing on fundamentals helps Paul Schmidlin (74) get to Michigan quarterback Dennis "The Menace" Brown.

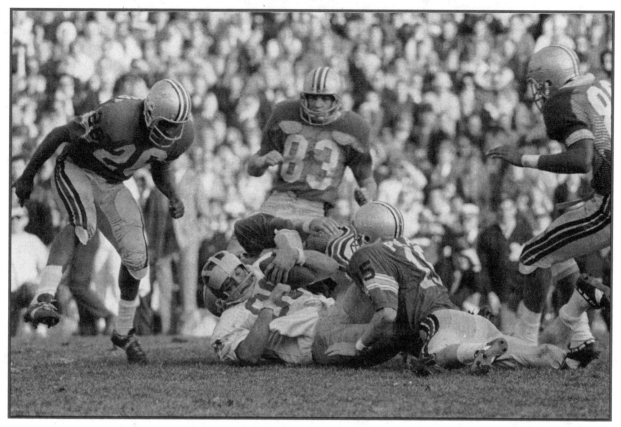

The triple-butt tackling drill of assistant coach Lou Holtz pays dividends as Mike Polaski (15), Mark Debevc (83) and Tim Anderson (26) close the road against Michigan.

arms out and get a stick. You peel around the pylons and come back and get a second stick, the same thing. Another form fit. Then you peel back off that for a third hit. The third hit is live for the tackler. The ball carrier still has to offer up the target. But on the third hit, when you hit him, you were supposed to drive your face mask through his chest, arm-grasp him, pull his legs into you, and bury him into the turf. I got the pleasure of doing this with Tatum, Anderson, Sensibaugh and Provost. *(Laughter.)* Man, at a hundred and fifty-eight pounds, this was a joy for me. I remember one situation where Tate was the ball carrier and T.A. was the tackler. And Timmy could uncork. Well, he fired on Tate, he hit him so hard that he snapped Tate's black leather belt we used to wear in our practice pants. Just broke it right in two in the back.

Smith: Those were great drills. You could kill somebody.

Jim Roman: Some things never change. I'm still using that drill (as a football coach)!

Stillwagon: You know what's amazing—I used to laugh—is if you could motivate people like they (coaches) did for orange drink. Wouldn't that be something! You remember the orange drink? (The equipment managers used to pass out ice-cold cartons of orange drink after practices.)

Everyone: Yeah, yeah, yeah.

Stillwagon: And if you could get a frozen juice, you'd just kill for it.

Donovan: Oh, those juices were valuable 'cause we didn't get any water at practice.

Stillwagon *(mimicking McCullough)***:** "Watah? You git that stuff outta heah!"

Nick Roman: Do you remember someone put tape remover in the hot tub?

Stillwagon: I remember Leo (Hayden) was in the hot tub once and he was putting his head down in the water going, "Vrooooom!" Everyone goes, "Leo! What are you doing?" He said, "I'm just playing." We said, "Do you know what's been in that tub?!?"

Zelina: John, do you remember the quarterback sneak play?

Muhlbach: Yes, I do. Rex would tap me

Jay Bombach
No. 48—Halfback

Mark Stier
No. 54—Linebacker

Vic Stottlemyer
No. 69—Guard

with his hand and I'd snap the ball then rather than waiting for the voice signals. We caught them off guard twice and Rex scored.

Otis: We had a bonfire on Friday night. And I had a kid come up to me at that bonfire and give me Bob Ferguson's chin strap.

Zelina: I think I remember that, Jim.

Otis: I showed Ernie Biggs (the late trainer) and told him that Bob Ferguson was supposed to have worn this chin strap against Michigan when he scored four touchdowns. So we taped it to the inside of my helmet because it didn't have a snap on it. The kid's name was Scooter, I think.

Zelina: I remember that now that you mention it because I was standing right next to you at the time.

Otis: You know that was a pretty tough game in the first half.

Zelina: I don't think we were thirty-six points better than they were.

Otis: Oh, no. Everything just gelled that game. I think it was 21-14 at the half and we had just scored just before the half. I think that this game was just a real, real tough hard hitting, great defensive ball game. Well, we had a great offensive game, too. ... You know, we had three backs in that game that out-rushed Ron

Gerald Ehrsam
No. 28—Defensive Halfback

Nicholas Roman
No. 89—End

Rufus Mayes
No. 73—Tackle

Alan Jack
No. 61—Guard

Dick Kuhn
No. 81—End

Thomas Backhus
No. 57—Guard

Johnson, Rex, you, and me. Again another great tailback that our defense stopped that year. You're talking about three top-notch (opponents), just as good as you could be in the country. ... That was probably, as I look back at that game, the most exciting time that I've ever had in my life as a football player. Just being there in that stadium, and they don't leave many seats for the Michigan people. ... You know the story about my last TD? You talked about Ray Gillian, he had a 50-yard run on the last drive. And by that time everyone's really out of the game. It's 44-14, and Ray takes the ball inside the 5. We're trying to score and, all of a sudden its fourth-and-2. And I'm standing

behind the Old Man and I said to him, "Do you want this TD?" He said, "Go on in." I said, "What play do you want?" He said, "You call it." So I get into the huddle and Dave Cheney is at left tackle. And I look right at Dave and said, "Cheney, Woody wants this going right over you and he expects us to get it. We ran the 27 and I go into the end zone. Bedlam broke loose. After all these years people still talk about us going for two points after the last TD. And it really wasn't Woody's fault. ... Doing something like that, being in line to be the national champion, does so much for the school and really a heck of a lot for the people living in the state. That's why it just kills me why these kids can't do it against Michigan.

Rex Kern
No. 10—Quarterback

David Brungard
No. 12—Halfback

James Otis
No. 35—Fullback

John Brockington
No. 42—Fullback

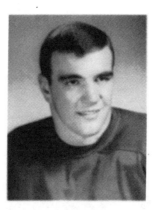

Paul Schmidlin
No. 74—Tackle

David Whitfield
No. 88—End

Tom Ecrement
No. 90—End

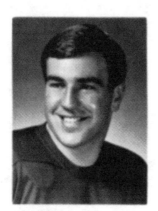

Butch Smith
No. 50—Linebacker

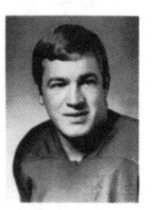

Mark Debevc
No. 83—Defensive End

OSU vs Michigan

SCORING

Michigan	7	7	0	0	—14
Ohio State	7	14	6	23	—50

MICH — Johnson, 1-yard run (Killian kick).
OSU — Otis, 5-yard run (Roman kick).
OSU — Kern, 5-yard run (Roman kick).
MICH — Johnson, 1-yard run (Killian kick).
OSU — Otis, 2-yard run (Roman kick).
OSU — Zelina, 6-yard run (kick failed).
OSU — Roman, 32-yard field goal.
OSU — Kern, 3-yard run (Roman kick).
OSU — Otis, 2-yard run (Roman kick).
OSU — Otis, 1-yard run (pass failed).
Attendance — 85,371

TEAM STATISTICS

	MICH	OSU
First downs	17	28
Rushing	41-140	79-421
Passing	14-24-171-3	9-6-46-1
Total yards	311	467
Punts-avg.	5-39.8	2-30.5
Punt returns	1-15	3-17
Kickoff returns	9-145	2-100
Int. returns	1-0	3-51
Fumbles-lost	5-1	4-2
Penalties-yards	4-43	4-37

CHAPTER THIRTEEN
Ohio State 27, Southern California 16

Rufus Mayes could see it coming. But the Ohio State offensive tackle only could watch helplessly as No. 2-rated Southern California's Heisman Trophy winner, O.J. Simpson, roared around and through the Ohio State defense for an 80-yard touchdown run to boost Southern California to a 10-0 lead in the second quarter of the fifty-fifth Rose Bowl at Pasadena, California. The only thing that could have stopped Simpson on that play, the stadium itself, did. Otherwise, he could have run all the way to the beach.

Staring at the scoreboard along with 102,063 fans and the largest international television audience ever to witness a college sporting event at that time, Mayes and his

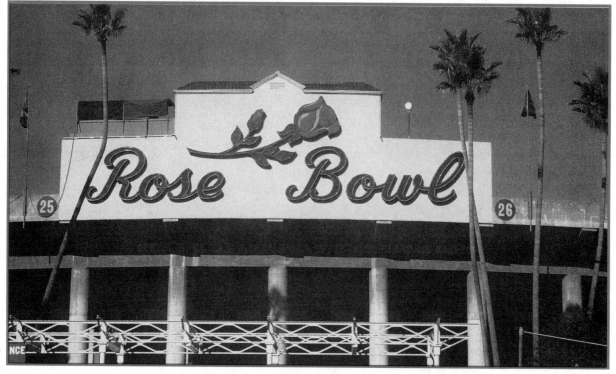

Any Big Ten Conference team will tell you THIS is the Promised Land.

teammates began to get fired up.

"There weren't many words when we got into the huddle," he said of the drive that began with about eight minutes left in the first half. "But I looked at the others and I could feel it.

"We're close. As close as brothers. I knew right then we'd get it back."

Even coach Woody Hayes was a believer. Asked about his feelings when the No. 1-ranked Buckeyes fell behind 10-0, the coach said: "I thought we'd win. Hell, yes. Oh, sure. Why? Because I felt we could move the ball on them. They took away our wide game, but to do it they put eight men up front and we hurt them with our passing and we could run inside.

"I felt if we could just play our football, we could still win."

In a big way. The Buckeyes piled up 260 yards and 16 first downs on the ground, led by fullback Jim Otis' 101 on 30 carries and half-back Leo Hayden's 90 on 15 carries.

The Buckeyes answered Simpson's run with a 1-yard run by Otis, capping a 13-play, 69-yard drive, and a 25-yard field goal by Jim Roman, at the end of a 54-yard march, to forge a 10-10 tie with three second left until halftime. The momentum, for however long Southern Cal might have had it, clearly shifted to the Buckeyes.

"That was as big as the devil," Hayes said of Roman's kick. "Say, we were a great field goal team today, weren't we?"

The defense, guided by coordinator Lou McCullough, was masterful in the second half. It made the offense's job much easier.

O.J. Simpson (32) shows the Buckeyes early in the game why he was the Heisman Trophy winner by taking off on an 80-yard touchdown run.

"We didn't give them good field position. We gave them great field position," McCullough said.

Said Hayes: "The biggest factor was our defense in the second half. O.J. broke loose for that big one in the first half, but we did a good job of stopping him in the second half. We did a good job of rushing (USC quarterback Steve) Sogge. We forced them into two fumbles and two interceptions. That's four turnovers, and the biggest thing was that we had no fumbles and no interceptions."

Rex Kern put on quite a show, one that eventually would secure the Most Valuable Player trophy for the Buckeyes' quarterback. His performance was all the more remarkable when one considers he missed ten practices in California with a shoulder injury, then suffered a shoulder separation during the game. But he guided OSU on a 12-play, 54-yard drive, capped by Roman's 25-yard field goal. Then, getting the ball back on the USC 21-yard line after defensive tackle Bill Urbanik pummeled USC quarterback Steve Sogge—causing a fumble which was recovered by middle guard Vic Stottlemyer—Kern drove the Scarlet and Gray to paydirt in five plays on a 4-yard pass to Hayden. The key play of the drive—Hayes said it possibly was the turning point of the game and, therefore, the season—was Kern's 14-yard scramble to the USC 4-yard line when he couldn't find an open receiver.

But it wasn't over. Safety Mike Polaski came up with Simpson's fumble at the Trojans' 16-yard line, and on the next play Kern connected with Ray Gillian for the touchdown. Gillian was in for wingback Larry Zelina, who sustained a cracked rib in the first half. Roman added his third conversion and ninth point. (To this day, Roman jokes that he, alone, outscored Simpson, 9-6.)

USC scored once more—on a disputed 19-yard pass from Sogge to Sam Dickerson—but it was of little consequence.

"Now let them vote," Kern shouted in the locker room just before the first of the No. 1 votes was cast. And it came from none other than No. 32, Simpson, who had entered the rowdy and jubilant OSU dressing quarters after rushing for 171 yards and catching eight passes for 85 yards.

"You're the best ball team in the country, and don't let anybody tell you that you aren't. Congratulations," Simpson said. With that, he was mobbed by Buckeyes for handshakes. Even Hayes made his way through the throng and stepped forward. "He's a real sportsman," the coach said.

Said Kern to his teammates upon receiving the MVP trophy: "Every part of this belongs to you guys." He finished 9-of-15 passing for 101

yards and the two scores, and he also had 35 yards rushing.

Hayes moderated a good-natured, spirited debate on who should receive the game ball.

"How about John Muhlbach? The little guy probably had his ankle fractured today," Hayes said. The players let out a collective groan.

"Doggone, he deserves it anyway," Hayes said.

Players started shouting nominations: Gillian, co-captain and offensive tackle Dave Foley, "all the seniors," senior linebacker Mark Stier (who had played with a badly injured shoulder) and others. Then Hayes cast another vote, this one for senior backup quarterback Bill Long, who had the mammoth touchdown run against Purdue and who had "been 'Steve Sogge'" all week against our defense.

"I guess we'll wind up giving about five," Hayes said.

And then it seemed as if the locker room nearly was empty. Ten games had come and gone. Just like that, the magic carpet ride was over. The ultimate goal of every college football

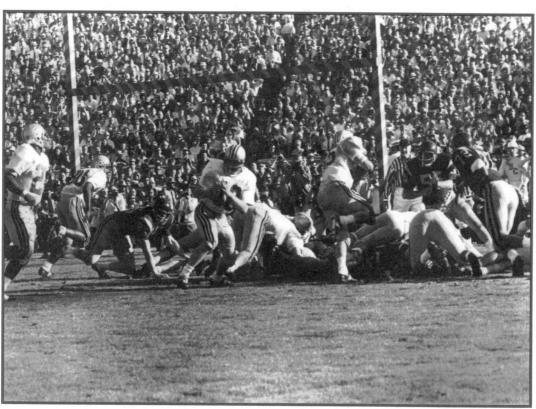

This 1-yard touchdown run by Jim Otis (35) is OSU's answer to Simpson's scoring run. Note how Rex Kern (10) and Leo Hayden (22) are deceptively "selling" the pitchout.

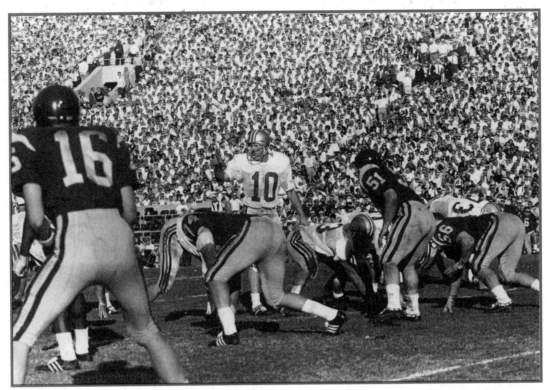

Rex Kern (10) changes a play at the line of scrimmage against the Trojans. His all-around effort would earn him the Most Valuable Player award for the game.

team had been attained by possibly one of the youngest teams ever to achieve it.

Hayes had sent his victorious troops off into the night with no curfew and with the next day off, except for a mandatory meeting at 9 p.m. After that, he was bound for Vietnam, where he would keep his promise to entertain U.S. service personnel.

Long after the players had left, Hayes, preparing to shower and head back to the hotel to take a call from President-elect Richard Nixon, was asked by Paul Hornung, sports editor of *The Columbus Dispatch,* if this represented his greatest victory.

"I suppose it was," he said. "Pretty convincing, wasn't it?"

That it was.

The post-game huddle

Zelina: Remember any stories about going out to the Rose Bowl?

Otis: Remember when we practiced in the French Fieldhouse? It was snowing and fairly

cold out back in Columbus, and Woody had it hot in the fieldhouse.

Zelina: It was hot, real hot.

Otis: He had it as hot as he could get it. He had those heaters going like nobody's business. And do you know what? Game day it was almost 90 degrees, about as hot as Woody had it in the fieldhouse. ... I think it's really tough for Midwest teams to go out to the Rose Bowl. Those guys don't have to do anything. They roll across the street and they are there.

Tatum: Going out to the Rose Bowl, that was the first time I had been to California. I remember landing and seeing palm trees for the first time. I said, "God, it's freezing back home and look at these palm trees ..."

Zelina: We went somewhere for a reception, and they gave us a bunch of oranges ...

Tatum: And we threw them back at the coaches because we were mad about getting taped on the plane and having to go practice as soon as we got there.

Stillwagon: We had a lot of good people and we had a lot of good players. Like you say, we pushed each other and we wanted to help each other. I think that sophomore year when we started out, I remember we played SMU, and Bill Mallory said, "We're gonna keep fresh troops in there the whole game. Don't worry; give it one hundred and ten percent." It was a wild, hot game and we won, and everybody (the coaches) said we played like crap. Every game we played that year, we played like crap. We won another one, we played like crap. We never should have won this one or that one. I remember (equipment manager John) Bozick saying, "You guys beat SMU; you never should have beaten them. Oregon should've kicked your butts. This was before Purdue, and I was getting my neck pulled out—I was over there getting some traction—and he goes, "This freakin' center from Purdue is gonna kill you." He says, "This guy is a piece of work." And I'm going, "Oh, forget you, Bozie." And then we kicked their butts, he said, "You guys are really pretty good." ... And then we get out to the Rose Bowl and we still had this tremendous, unknown energy. They (the coaches) kicked the tar out of us at the Rose Bowl (practices). I remember Bill Urbanik and myself chased

Gerry Ehrsam—remember that pursuit thing, where you had to touch him?—and we chased him across the tennis court onto another baseball field, and Bill was going *(He pantomimes gasps for breath to the delight of those in the room.)* ... They finally broke us up and Gerry Ehrsam looks up and says, "I'm just doing what they told me to do." ...

Zelina: What about Brad?

Stillwagon: Brad Nielsen, I'll never forget, he rushed and he got to Sogge. And the big tackle turned on the center ...

Nick Roman: Yary? Ron Yary?

Stillwagon: That might've been it. He said, "I'm gonna kick your butt, you so-and-so, if you ever let these guys in here again." And they start fighting, and Brad looks at me and says, "We'd better get the heck out of here. These guys turn on us, they'll kick our butts!" ... I always think about Brad. You know, you think about the players, and everybody played a vital role. Everybody was treated—as I see it, anyway—the same. Everybody had different feelings, maybe, but everybody wanted to be treated the same. We had great feelings toward

Ohio State faithful offer a suggestion to the Buckeyes' defense.

With Rex Kern making a point, Woody Hayes listens to a suggestion from the press box.

each other. There wasn't an elitist group. It was fun, and when we did things together everybody was happy. ... This 1968 team, it was a thing that happened stage, by stage, by stage.

Otis: I thought our defense was spectacular in that game. Again, we bent a little bit. But, man, did they finish strong!

Zelina: Offensively, you and Leo had great games. And Ray Gillian had a great game, and Rex had a great game. When we finally buttoned it down, you carried five or six times in a row just to get us started. Then we broke Leo for a couple nice gains.

Otis: That was probably Leo's best game of the year.

Zelina: The two of you absolutely pounded them to death. And USC had some great athletes on that team.

Tatum: You talk about another guy stepping up, Ray Gillian comes in and steps up big time.

Zelina: Comes in and has a huge game, I mean a huge game! I got my ribs broken the

last play of the first quarter. I was running a little curl down on the goal line and Rex overthrew me and I went up and one of their linebackers caught me with his helmet right in the ribs. In that game I didn't wear rib pads, I didn't wear hip pads, I didn't wear anything because I wanted to be quick. So I get my ribs broken and Ray came in and darn near was the MVP!

Tatum: Yeah, he had a great game.

Zelina: It's like some of the things that weren't talked about. When you have so many good athletes and there's so much competition at every position, you have great athletes that didn't get the opportunity to play as much as they should have.

Tatum: I'll tell you one thing I remember about that game. They were going in to score and threw a little swing pass to O.J., and I caught up with him and knocked him out of bounds on the 2- or 3-yard line. And we held them there. Baugh made two or three big stops in a row and we stop them. What people don't know about that play is O.J. was my guy. We had a little mix-up on defense and I'm standing there, and O.J. swings out and I'm standing there covering the tackle. Well, I thought he was the tight end at first—because I was talking, and when I turned around he's supposed to be the tight end. But he wasn't. So I'm standing there and O.J. swings out and I'm thinking, That's my guy. I'd better get him.

Zelina: That probably was the quickest I ever saw you move.

Tatum: I had to get him because I screwed up totally.

Zelina: That turned the game around. That hit and Sensibaugh's big stops turned it around. They wind up settling for a field goal. We turn around and take the ball down the field and score.

Tatum: It was a great game. It didn't hit me until we were back at the hotel what we had done. I remember O.J. coming into our locker room after the game and congratulating us, and I thought that was a classy move on his part. ... It's funny, you know. He broke that one long run against us, but with all the hype about O.J. and everything I wasn't disappointed that he did that. That kind of said that he was a great player because no one ran through us like that. It was like, "Well he got his one big run," but we stopped him the rest of the day. Fumbled twice in the second half. He was supposed to be a great player and it was kind of good to see him be a great player. Then you can say that you beat the best. ... I'll tell you what's really special: A lot of times I go out and I talk to kids and stuff and I'll be telling them something and it'll hit me, Man, you sound just like Woody. You know? And it's things that he told us, points that he made to us. One of the things that he always said was, "Look around. These guys are going to be your best friends for the rest of your life. And I found that to be true. Even living in California, I still keep in touch with (Ralph) Holloway, (John) Hicks, and as many guys as I can. These guys are better friends than a lot of guys I met in the pros. I think it's because we kind of grew up together.

Otis: That was the perfect game. One team was ranked No. 1 and the other was No. 2. That's what they're trying to do now (with the Bowl Alliance). I think what happened was we

hadn't played in a month and USC had gotten to play after we did (the week after Michigan). They usually had some late games. And it just took us awhile to get our motors running. ... I'll tell you one thing, our team was in shape. We wore them out in the second half. We ran them right out of the Rose Bowl.

Polaski: Hey, remember this? We go to the Rose Bowl, and Rufe (Rufus Mayes) goes downtown and goes to a pawn shop. And Rufe's got a lot—at that time it was a lot of money—to buy a camera to take to the Rose Bowl. He wanted to take pictures to remember his trip by. And he's got the whole thing. He's got the thirty-five-millimeter camera. He's got the carrying case. The whole shot. Big shoulder bag hanging down, and we're at Disneyland. We're walking, and this little kid, probably six or seven years old, goes by with his dad. Of course, Rufus, at that time was a huge man. This kid looks at Rufus, then looks at his dad, then looks back at Rufus and says, "Dad! Dad! Look at the big colored kid with the purse!" And Rufus turns and looks at me and says, "Ski, only me. I just spent a hundred and fifty dollars on a camera to be called a big colored kid with a purse!"

Muhlbach: Oranges. You know what I remember about going out there? They had the Rose Bowl queen and her court up there, and, like we talked about, somebody make the mistake of giving us oranges. And Mallory stood up and said something, and everybody started throwing oranges at him. And they wiped out the court and the queen.

Polaski: And I remember the first practice we had. We thought it was going to be Picture Day.

Nick Roman: Oh! Ha, ha, ha! It was Media Day!

Polaski: They decided they were gonna show the guys on the West Coast that we were the meanest bastards that ever set foot out there. ... And remember, we couldn't go to the Lawry's Beef Bowl because they were "trying to fatten us up?"

Zelina: Everything that they did out there was supposed to be "against us." They had this big Lawry's Beef Bowl where the teams would come in and see who could eat the most beef, and Woody wouldn't let us go.

Polaski: I want to tell you the truth. If we hadn't won that football game, that would have been the worst two weeks of my entire life. We busted our butts out there. That was nothing but plain, old hard work, and winning the ball game, thirty years later, makes it all worthwhile.

Zelina: I think we really showed our character that game because we were never down in a game that year other than Northwestern early, but never down to a strong team by ten points. We didn't fold. We did NOT fold!

Otis: I can tell you this for a fact. I was one of the lucky guys who got to play football a little longer than some guys did. And I can tell you this, that Ohio State team, I loved every guy on that team and I knew it was never going to be the same. Playing in the pros was never, ever the same. With all the tradition at Ohio State and having a coach like we had, everybody cared about each other. It's not like that in the pros. When I was with the (St. Louis) Cardinals, that was the closest it came. My time at Ohio State with that team will always be the fondest of memories. There's just nothing else that could take its place.

How do you like us now?

OSU vs Southern California

SCORING

Ohio State	0	10	3	14	—27
USC	0	10	0	6	—16

USC — Ayala, 21-yard field goal.

USC — Simpson, 80-yard run (Ayala kick).

OSU — Otis, 1-yard run (Roman kick).

OSU — Roman, 25-yard field goal.

OSU — Hayden, 4-yard pass from Kern (Roman kick).

OSU — Gillian, 16-yard pass from Kern (Roman kick).

USC — Dickerson, 19-yard pass from Sogge (pass failed).

Attendance — 102,063

TEAM STATISTICS

	OSU	USC
First downs	21	19
Rushing	67-260	42-177
Passing	9-15-101-0	19-32-189-2
Total yards	361	366
Punting average	45.6	36.9
Punt returns	3-20	5-35
Kickoff returns	4-45	6-84
Int. returns	2-22	0-0
Fumbles-lost	1-0	3-1
Penalties-yds.	6-53	3-51

CHAPTER FOURTEEN
The Assistants Have Their Say

You've read about our exploits during that perfect championship season. Remember how we said we were as prepared, or better prepared, than any team we faced? That's a credit to the coaching staff.

I asked Earle Bruce, an offensive line coach for us, George Chaump, the quarterbacks coach, Lou McCullough, our defensive coordinator and Lou Holtz, the defensive backs coach, to relive the 1968 season. Please enjoy the transcripts of those discussions.

- L.Z.

■■■

EARLE BRUCE
Offensive line

Zelina: You came here in 1966?

Bruce: Yes, Mallory came in 1966, then I came. George Chaump came in 1968.

Zelina: What did you think of that coaching staff?

Bruce: That coaching staff was great. Do you know what the greatest thing was about that staff? We all worked together and we didn't worry at all about what anyone did.

Some coaching staffs you get on, coaches are always worried about getting ahead, who's going to get the next job. That was never an issue with that staff. Just do your job the best you can. I will say, though, that you were happy as could be when Woody was on some other coach. When he was on Mallory, I was happy, but when he got on my butt, Mallory was happy.

Zelina: Mallory, Holtz, McCullough, Sark ...

Bruce: I have to laugh because I tell Holtz all the time how lucky he was to have been here just one year and to be associated with our national championship. You don't get to know Coach Hayes from one year of coaching defense. Coach under Woody for six years like I did. I'd tease him—have Woody be on your butt a whole year, you would really know what it's all about.

Zelina: How hard was it to get Woody to change his mind about the offensive scheme?

Bruce: I wanted to run the I (formation), Woody didn't want to run the I. Well, yes, George and I were in favor of the I, and I think Woody was ready to change. There was great feeling among the staff to go to the I-formation and to feature the tailback as well as the fullback. We ran the ball, I mean we ran the ball, shoot we could run the ball!

Do you know that Woody came in as a passing coach? And then earned a reputation (for) three yards and a cloud of dust. You know what? Football is really a 10-yard game if anybody really studies it. When you talk about it, ten yards, three downs, three-and-a-third yards a down, and you keep the ball. Then you play strong defense and you win the football game. That's what it was supposed to be all about. Football was supposed to be a toughness sport. Now they're making it a doggone basketball game. Always taking shots from mid-court.

Zelina: I think I'm hearing a little Big Ten philosophy now.

Bruce: I've gotta be honest with you. I study the stats all the time and if you look at the Big Ten record book, you talk about quarterbacks, running backs, whatever, from 1978 to 1986 (and) that league was really blessed with a lot of talent.

Zelina: What did you think of the talent on the 1968 team?

Bruce: Oh, my God, what an array of talent! You take the 1968 team, but I'll tell you what, the 1969 team was even better. We lost to Michigan in 1969 and I hate to say this, if it was anybody's fault we lost to Michigan in 1969, it was Woody's. The 1969 team was the greatest team I ever saw at Ohio State. When I came to OSU in 1966 I was appalled at the lack of talent. I told Woody that I had three or four players at Massillon (High School) who could play here, and two of them did, Dave Whitfield and John Muhlbach. We had a mental problem in 1966 and 1967, although in 1967 they saved our jobs.

Zelina: That came up in talking with the players in our roundtable discussions—how we came in as freshmen in 1967 and practiced against the varsity and by the end of the year we were beginning to know each other and feel good about each other. And remember the battles we used to wage and I think it paid off for them near the end of that year when all the coaches' jobs were on the line if we didn't win out?

Bruce: You know what? I gotta tell you this story; you probably remember it. I was defensive backfield coach in 1967 and I had a little tackling drill for the defensive backs, and you guys would come over and run the ball

against us and I'd put three guys up against you freshmen backs and all three of those guys would wind up on the ground looking up. And I'd say, "Geez, we can't tackle!"

Zelina: When did you sense the potential was there?

Bruce: Oh, God, the athletic talent was there; we saw that when you guys were freshmen. Man, we were hoping we could survive. When they told us we might get fired in 1967 we said, "Oh, God, we won't have a shot with these guys. We didn't know it was gonna be in 1968, but we knew the potential was there for something great. We had talent. I mean, we had great talent. We had kids that liked to play the game, I mean crazy guys, but guys that liked to play the game.

Zelina: Give me a few thoughts on the Purdue game.

Bruce: Do you remember how big that Purdue team was? Let me tell you what our plan was. With those two big guys over our guards, our guards cut them. Their butts were on the ground more than you've seen anybody on the ground. They just went after their legs and tied their legs up. They did a heckuva job. They had a middle guard, I don't remember his name. Woody had tried to recruit him, said he was a great all-around athlete. He was a big factor in Purdue's defense, and we handled him. The big play was the interception by Provost that was run back for a touchdown, when he jumped the out-cut by Keyes. ... If I remember correctly, Holtz and Hugh Hindman had a hundred-dollar bet. Holtz said that they'd intercept a pass and run it in for a TD. And he (Holtz) was figuring on doing that, and Hugh said they wouldn't do that. I remember that. He had to pay him off.

Zelina: Do you remember when we went to the unbalanced line in the Michigan game?

Bruce: Do I remember? What are you talking about? My guards beat the crap out of everybody that game.

Zelina: I still say we had the finest pair of pulling guards in the country.

Bruce: Oh, my God, did we! We had six of them that could play! Backhus, Alan Jack, Strickland, Donovan, Kurz ...

Zelina: You had some great teams, some real good, quality teams during your head coaching at OSU and got close to No. 1 a couple times.

Bruce: But we never had all the talent. But you know what? When you're in that situation—like the 1968, 1969, 1970 teams—with the players there was a special chemistry. That they like each other, they run around together, be with each other, they play together and they have a sense that when they walk out on the football field they're gonna get the job done. They're gonna perform. It was a really—what do you say—joy to coach and trouble-free, know what I mean? Weren't any really great problems. We just tended to business and coached and enjoyed it. The players all just seemed to, and the coaches, we just had a bond. It was so nice it was unbelievable, you know?

Zelina: It was the only coaching staff I was ever exposed to for an extended time, but we felt like the coaches were our friends.

Bruce: You know what? All the guards and centers used to come over and sit on my patio and we used to laugh and joke—and you know what? They enjoyed football and they enjoyed being around each other and I enjoyed not only having them in my home on Thursday nights, but I enjoyed having them come to my office and sitting down and looking at the film and talking football. I want to tell you something: I had more arguments about grades when it came grade time (for game films) than anytime I've ever had. If I graded one low, aw, man, they'd ask about it. But everything seemed to mesh really well. Especially, like you mentioned, it really gelled after we beat Purdue. It let us know that we were for real and we could do something if we kept working hard. Everything seemed to be there, although like every team has to get through a pitfall, and Illinois was a pitfall, and we had to come through at the end and win. And even though they were not a good football team when we went there, we came through with a victory— but it was by the skin of our teeth. We didn't play exceptionally well and at Iowa almost the same thing. We won and we didn't play as well as we could, but they had a good football team and no one took account. Playing them there was really something. And when you come down to the Michigan game, and that's when

it's all on the line. ... I think early in the ball game it's 14-14, and all of a sudden roof caved in and at halftime it was 21-14. And in the second half it was all over. I knew that they had cashed in their chips.

Zelina: It seemed like it all came together.

Bruce: It was like icing on the cake.

Zelina: Jim Roman says us going for two points late in the Michigan game was as a result of the kicking game. Others say Woody said he went for two because they wouldn't let him go for three. What do you recall?

Bruce: Let me tell you something ... what I know about it. I know that Otis came out of the ball game yelling, "Run the ball, run the ball, run for two, get fifty." We heard Woody say, "Well, let's run it. And holy shoot, we're up in the press box yelling, "No, no, don't do that! Please don't do that!" Because we knew what that meant; we didn't know that Elliott would get fired and Bo (Schembechler) would come in, but we knew they'd use that to motivate their football team. He didn't realize at the time what a motivational thing that could, would become. I knew it was wrong going for two at that point just to get fifty points.

Zelina: The players have had their laughs about getting taped on the plane on the way out to the Rose Bowl. Did you know that was going to happen?

Bruce: Did we know? Absolutely not! The real story was in 1970, when he did the same doggone thing. And he promised we wouldn't do it. Aw, I laughed; I couldn't believe it. I remember the meeting, deciding we wouldn't tape on the plane. I remember the coaches were sitting in the back of the plane playing cards with match sticks and everything and someone came back and said, "Do you realize he's taping us? He's taping us!" We told whoever to go talk to (Hayes), to tell him the plan was not to tape, but to have a day of relaxation. That first year at the Rose Bowl was something else. We would practice. We came back from practice, he had a press conference, he'd take a long time at the press conference, we went in and started eating. He'd come in during the middle of the meal. He'd start eating. He'd take forever to eat. Everybody would sit there until he would tell them to go. And he'd just keep eating slower and slower, making them wait.

And I could see everybody getting antsy. And then he'd say, "Okay, you can go." So you'd have an hour and a half to leave Pasadena to go to Hollywood — or wherever you went — and get back. It was unbelievable. You guys would travel an hour to spend forty-five minutes seeing everything you possibly could. He had it planned that way.

Zelina: There were some athletes on USC's team.

Bruce: Absolutely. They had a great offensive line. I'll tell you one thing: They jumped off to a 10-0 lead and we came back and tied it and then won it, 27-16. It should have been 27-10, but that official gave them their last TD on that blown call in the end zone. I thought it was a great game that we played. Muhlbach broke his leg in the second quarter, I think, and Roman played the rest of the way.

That was an enjoyable year to coach, and not only because of the great talent and the way the season played out. It was such a joy, like you said—the people coming in and the coaches and watching the film. They even came when they didn't have to come. Most players don't go around the coaches' offices when they don't have to. They stay clear of the coaches sometimes. I thought it was doggone good the way the guys came around and spent some time.

Zelina: You talked about it a little while ago, but the guys still remember the Thursday nights at your house. Holtz and McCullough did the same thing with their guys.

Bruce: You know who loved it more than anybody? My kids. My two little girls. That was a big night for them. My kids were only eight and six, or something like that, but I'll tell you, they were really into it. It was something to behold.

■■■

GEORGE CHAUMP
Quarterbacks

Zelina: How much of our offense did you put in?

Chaump: It was a change of philosophy. We would spread a guy out, we used a wideout, we threw the ball more. I think by the end of

the 1968 season, we had about every offensive record at OSU. But it was not just plays, it was a system. Woody still kept the Robust (full-house backfield with two tight ends) and quite honestly it was good for us, because if we got inside the 20-yard line, nobody ever stopped us. Great short-yardage offense the way we ran it, and the way Woody knew it. That played a large part of our success, not to diminish Woody's contribution—because I think we did need the Robust offense and it did complement the other. ... Everybody contributed ... I probably was the pioneer of change.

Zelina: How did it come about?

Chaump: The first responsibility I had when I came to OSU was to study game film of the freshmen. This was late winter 1968. All the other coaches were busy recruiting, and Woody told me since I was coming in from a high school position I wouldn't know anything about recruiting. So he asked me to analyze the freshman films, and I did. As a matter of fact, I broke them down, and made notes and everything else because he wanted me to report back to him on personnel, evaluate the individual players and what I thought. So the coaches got back from recruiting and we're getting ready for spring practice of 1968. So I'm in my first coaches' meeting and Woody goes to the board and writes ROBUST. ... He said he called this offense Robust because it means big and strong. That name took on a national meaning because he talked at clinics across the country about his offensive philosophy. So he starts talking about the fullback play, and I said to myself, Boy, what a formation this guy's running; he coaches in a phone booth with everybody bunched up so tight. It doesn't use the field or spread the field and he wouldn't use the talent we have that well. I got concerned. I didn't think this would work well with the talent I saw on film. But he was dead set with fullback, fullback, fullback. I had come off of a high school team where we threw the ball and used the whole field. My last four high school teams had won four straight "PA" state championships. I was pretty much into the throwing game if I had a quarterback, and I thought we had those types of quarterbacks here at OSU.

Zelina: You also liked the I-formation.

Chaump: Yes, I did. So here's what happened then. I listened to him in the coaches' meeting the first day. And the second day we're still covering different ways of running the fullback off tackle. So I went out to lunch with the other assistant coaches, and I asked them if this was how Coach Hayes runs his meetings? We had no input up to this time and I wanted to know if we could ask questions. And Hugh Hindman said, "Sure, you can ask questions." Earle and the other coaches said, "Sure, go ahead and ask some questions if you want to." They were setting me up, of course. So we get back from lunch and Woody again goes into the same stuff. And I'm getting a little nervous again over what I'm hearing. I finally raise my hand, and Woody wants to know what's on my mind. I said, "Coach, can I ask a question or two? He said, "Sure, what is it?" I said, "Is this what we're going to use as our basic offensive formation?" And he said, "Well, yeah, unless you think you know something better." Well, I got a little bit humble and said, "Coach, I don't know if it's better but I do have some ideas that I'd like to talk about a little bit." (Hayes asks:) "Well, what's that?" I said, "Are we going to utilize our offense best from this formation?" He said, "Why do you ask?" I said, "Well, you gave an assignment to look at films of freshmen and I did. And I saw everything was run from a straight-T (formation) and I said, 'My, I wonder what we could do if we could just split these guys out, because I saw great talent on that team. I think if we split them out I think we could move the ball better.' So Woody asked me, "What do you have in mind?' And I said, "The guy you're putting at tight end, Jan White, I had him in high school, and I think you have other guys you can do this with. I think we can do some things where we'd be a little more open." Woody said, "What would you do?" I said, "The first thing I'd do is split a wideout out there and I'd throw the ball to him and force double coverage on him by the defense." He said, "What would you throw him?" I said, "A little 5-yard out pass we call the Jet cut." I showed him how we'd do it, and we talked a long while on all the details of the Jet cut, which was so simple. I said, "But what I'm trying to do is force double coverage out there and that will give us an advantage blocking inside. Now we can run the ball with a seven-

man front, which we could run from a tight slot with a wingback." So he finally asked me, "What plays would you run? What would your first running play be?" I said, "Well, I always like the off-tackle play." He said, "How would you run it?" I said, "Coach, we got in the I-formation and we ran both sides. To the tight end side we'd double-team with the tight end and tackle. To the wingback side, we'd double-team with the wingback and tackle. Then, we'd kick out with the fullback, we pulled our backside guard around and led, we reversed pivot and gave the ball deep to our tailback and ran off tackle either way." Well, Woody said, "Let me tell you about that play. I was an analyst for the USC-Notre Dame game, and USC was running that play and ND was smashing them. Heck, all you've got there is a glorified guard playing fullback. He's telling those linebackers where the ball is going and they're licking their chops! Furthermore, the tailback is six yards deep, and by the time they get to the line the linebackers are there and they're whacking him. I'll tell you about that play: It's about as subtle as slicing bread with a baseball bat. That formation is nothing but a lighthouse formation. You've got two guys standing and everybody sees where they're going on the defense." He said, "As long as I'm head coach of football at Ohio State, nobody is going to take away my fullback play. Now do you think your play is better than the fullback off-tackle play?" And I made the mistake of saying, "Coach, there's no comparison." He said, "WHAT?" I said, "Coach, on the tailback play you have a double-team, you have a kickout, you have a guard leading through and you've got a tailback carrying the ball that should be faster than your fullback. You can run it to both sides and it's a much better play because of the power you generate." Well, Woody started blowing a fuse and says to me, "You mean you're standing here telling me that the power off-tackle play is better than the fullback play?" I said, "Yes, sir." He said, "That's it! Get the heck out! Get out of here! Anyone who doesn't like to run the fullback doesn't coach football at Ohio State! You're fired! Get out of here!" I thought he was kidding, so I stayed there and he said, "I'm serious! Get out of here!" Well, I didn't know him that well, so I got my notebook and I walked out thinking to myself, I just started a new job, open my mouth once and I get fired. Now I'm second-guessing everything I'm doing. All of a sudden the meeting room door flies open and Woody sticks his head out and says, "Get back in here. I've never fired a coach yet and I'm not going to start with you. So get back in here and listen." So I went back in and sat. Meanwhile, none of the other coaches had said anything before. They kind of left me hanging. Once I got back in the room, I remember Hugh Hindman speaking up. He said, "Coach, I know you get mad and I know there may be things you don't want to hear, but I think there's some things you've got to hear. You know, we almost got fired last year and things are a little bit tight. You can be mad if you want, but I think we should talk about changing some things. Personally, I like some of the things I heard." Then I think Earle Bruce chimed in and said, "Coach, he's right. We've got to do something different." Tiger Ellison, the silver-tongued orator, he gave out a rebel call: "Yahoo! Shades of run-and-shoot." He was a run-and-shoot disciple. So this is all fascinating. And I'll never forget this: Woody got quiet. It was like an about-face. It was like all the blood ran out of his face and he got kind of meek. And he said, "Well, well, if we're going to talk about it, we better get started." So we talked a little bit more and Woody asked who's running this stuff? Well, Oklahoma; Arkansas, where Frank Broyles was coaching; USC, where John McKay was coach, and they were all I-formation teams. I had heard them all speak at clinics. I traveled all over the country listening to coaches at clinics and I got it from them. So Woody said we'd better get their films and look at them and study them. Well, we did that. And Woody made us get graph paper and diagram all the plays I was talking about according to the width of the field in proportion to the graph paper. We'd be at the office until one in the morning. And Hugh and Earle and Rudy would look at me and say, "You no good so-and-so. We're all here because of you. It's your fault." You know what, Larry? We changed, and you know the rest of the story. That's all true and that's what happened. That's how we got into the "I" and slot "I." So Woody said we're still going to run the Robust in short-yardage and goal-line (situations). Ultimately, both offenses complemented each other and the Robust was a great weapon with the personnel we had. We had pretty good kids and we pounded people. We had good fullbacks and good tailbacks. And we threw the ball.

Zelina: So you weathered the storm and headed into spring ball with a new offensive scheme.

Chaump: I'll tell you a story about the very first spring practice for me at college. We're all excited, and Woody wants to meet with the players before we went out on the field. We met in the meeting room at the North Facility. It was fascinating. Woody talked about practice and he talked about the season coming up, and for some reason he was obsessed with Purdue. They had beaten us badly the year before. Badly. It was 35-0 at halftime and (Jack) Mollenkopf was their coach and he sat along the sideline and he had a hat on as he sat in his seat the whole second half, and he pulled his hat down over his eyes. And the film was shot across the field from where he was. After every play you could see Mollenkopf there. Woody would look at that film and the score and it would drive Woody crazy. That whole meeting Woody lectured and talked about "those guys, Purdue, we're gonna beat those so-and-sos. ... And at the end, if you guys don't beat them on the field, I'm gonna get that old coach of theirs and I'll challenge him on the 50-yard line and I'll beat him up!" With that, Woody grabbed some picture and threw it up against the wall and it smashed. He had guys running out of that locker room. I'm saying, "Holy cow! Is this the first day of spring practice?" I thought we were going out to play for the national championship.

Zelina: Purdue became an obsession with Woody.

Chaump: He talked about beating Purdue, and I tell you, he planted that seed. I guess this was the mastery of Woody. Because we beat Purdue and I think that Purdue was the consensus No. 1 team at the time. I don't think there was a sports writer in America that picked us to beat Purdue. It was the upset of the century. That night they shut down High Street. The kids were down there and they tore the place apart.

Zelina: You were hired as the quarterbacks coach.

Chaump: We had a great QB group, Rex and Mace, and of course, Billy Long and Kevin Rusnak. My biggest job was to try and keep those boys happy, keep their morale up and make them feel like they were all a part of it.

Zelina: Your first game as an OSU coach was against SMU. Remember any highlights?

Chaump: Brungard ran a blast play where he was stopped, bounced outside, broke some tackles, and took it all the way. I remember later that Davey and Woody had a falling out, and Dave transferred to Alabama the next year. It was a shame because Dave's father was a good player at Ohio State. Dave Brungard was a great guy and a heckuva ball player, too. I think he was co-captain at Alabama his senior year.

Zelina: The game of the year was against Purdue. As quarterbacks coach, do you remember the big play?

Chaump: Rex Kern gets hurt, and we're down around the 12-yard line, and Woody puts Billy Long in and everybody starts booing. I don't think they were booing Billy, I think they were booing Woody for taking Kern out. First play, Bill goes back to pass, it was a delay to the wingback. He sees an opening, he takes off, he runs and scores. That's how we score our TD. Biggest play of the season. After we beat them, no one would come close to us because we were all solidified and the chemistry was right and our kids were confident. And we just went crazy.

Zelina: Jankowski caught a TD pass. Your offense started showing.

Chaump: It wasn't my offense. We got it from other people. ... But I was the guy who started it at OSU.

Zelina: Tell me about our trip to Champaign, our first road trip.

Chaump: I remember Woody taking us to the same restaurant he always took the team to when they went to Illinois. The restaurant was beautiful, and Woody, as he always did, had this elderly waiter there who had a wonderful baritone voice. Well, the waiter sang three songs, and before we left, Woody offered any one of us who could name all three songs a dollar bill. Woody also gave a speech about Abraham Lincoln, since he came from that part of the country. Woody said Lincoln would have made a heck of a tackle!

Zelina: Rex got hurt in the Michigan State game and Mace started against Wisconsin. Tell me something about Mace.

Chaump: He was called the Super Sub. Every time Rex got hurt, Mace went in and did a heckuva job. He was so good coming in that role. He just had a knack for being the relief pitcher and coming in and doing well. I don't know what it was. ... They were two great guys to have on the team. And I loved that little Kevin Rusnak, because he was a frisky little bugger from Garfield, New Jersey.

Zelina: You kept those QBs up because it was pretty tough for them with Woody in the middle of the huddle all the time.

Chaump: It was hard to play QB if you didn't have a sense of humor. I loved those guys. I'd have to get out on the field a half hour early and stay out a half hour late. It was murder. We'd be out there throwing until their arms were ready to fall off, and then we wouldn't throw much in a game—and I'd feel so bad.

Zelina: Do you remember what Woody used to tell us about the passing game? Even with you there pushing it, he still didn't like the passing game.

Chaump: Oh, yeah. He'd say, "When you throw the darned ball, three things could happen and two of them are bad." He said, "Even *you* can figure out the percentages aren't too good. Number one, you can have it intercepted; that's horrible. Number two, it can be incomplete. And number three, you can catch it. Now, two out of three are bad." I think he forgot one thing: You can get sacked, and that's bad. If you look at it that way, its three out of four are bad. ... Woody was a trip. He ran that fullback play all the time. He just ran it all the time. I asked why he ran it so much. And he said in a very smart and sarcastic way, "I'll tell you why. I want to keep running that play until I get it just right." I said, "There's no deception to it. They see the fullback going boom-boom." He said, "B.S. There's no deception." He said, "It's the most deceptive play in the game." He said our fullback lines up right behind the ball. And the other team doesn't know if he's going to go right or left. That was Woody's idea of deception. ... Do you remember the time in practice when we completed nine passes in a row. I used to hate practice in the spring, because it was such a windy season. It was usually cold and windy and miserable to throw in. I could see why Woody hated the pass so much. I remember at the North Facility we had nine in a row one day. And after nine in a row, Rex throws an interception. Now you know how Woody despised an interception. And Woody goes into a tantrum. He gets all the QBs together and tells them, "You're not going to play at OSU if you throw interceptions." He says, "All of you! I want you to run all the way down to the fence, touch it, and run all the way back." Remember the fence way down there about four football fields away, and there was a McDonald's on the other side of the fence? So, the QBs start running, and Woody turns and looks at me and says, "Shoot, you're their coach, you run with them." So I said, "Heck, I'll run with them." And we take off running, the QBs and me. We were laughing, you know, Kern and Mace and Rusnak and Long and me. And I told them if we could get through that fence I'd buy them all a hamburger. I made fun of it just to keep them all loose. So we ran down and back. And the next day at practice, that doggone Rex, he put a pair of sneakers in my locker just in case we had to do some more running together.

Zelina: Would you tell the story about the coaches' meeting when Woody was checking on the players' grades?

Chaump: That's where you got a special nickname. Woody always was on the coaches to make sure that their respective players were doing what they should be doing in the classroom as well as the football field. If you coached a player and he was screwing up in the classroom, you were in trouble. It wasn't the player's fault, it was your fault as a coach. And if a player wasn't doing well, you had to stay on him. Woody didn't expect us as coaches to just tell him about it, but have the players in your office studying. So there was this pretty good back from up in Cleveland who got off to a shaky start with the books and I was told about it when I joined the staff. This situation takes place in spring of 1968 just before practice was going to start. It was grade time and Woody was concerned how some of the guys

were doing. His biggest drive was to keep every player healthy and keep every player in school. Woody was ahead of everybody in that academic respect. So he was asking about the players, and I'll be darned, the first guy he questions is me. He says, "George?" And he caught me a little off guard. I think I was daydreaming about back home and I was a little homesick in Ohio. My wife was back in Harrisburg; he caught me off guard. He said, "What can you tell me about Zelina? And I tried to deceive him to buy a little more time. So I said, "Zelina ... Zelina ... Larry Zelina?" And Woody said, "No, doggone it, Bobo Zelina! Who the heck do you think I'm talking about?" He caught me flat-footed, and I stuttered and stammered. So to your teammates you might have been Z-Man, but from that moment on to the coaches who were in that room you were Bobo!

Zelina: What was the most important thing you had to accomplish your first year at OSU?

Chaump: I had to learn Woody. I didn't know him. I was the only coach ever at that time that was a high school coach that was put on the staff that was from out of state. It was Earle Bruce, I think, that went to bat for me and I got the job. I had a lot of great players in high school. Dennis Green was a tailback. he's now the coach of the Minnesota Vikings. ... I'll tell you a good story. Lou Holtz was on the staff, and we're getting ready to play Purdue. Everybody's worried sick. It was Thursday night and I remember Hugh Hindman saying, "Well, are we ready?" And Lou said, "You better believe we're ready." Hugh asked him, "Do you think we can stop Phipps' passes?" Lou said, "We're going to shut them out." Hugh said, "I tell you what, Lou. You shut them out, and I'll give you one hundred dollars. At that time, one hundred dollars was a lot of money. We shut them out, by golly, and Hugh gave Lou one hundred dollars. Lou still has that hundred framed, signed by Hugh, on his wall.

Zelina: When did you finally feel comfortable about your decision to come to OSU as an assistant coach?

Chaump: After the Rose Bowl, Woody was getting ready to go to Vietnam to visit the troops there, and we were going to stay behind to go to the coaches' convention in L.A. The convention wasn't until a week later, so rather than fly back to Columbus we said we'd just go to Las Vegas for a few days and then go right back to L.A. for the convention. Which we did. So we were going there and that morning before Woody left, we're all feeling good, popping our chests out. We're national champs! And in my own personal life, that was the fifth straight year I came off a team that was undefeated! My last four in high school and my first one at Ohio State. Now we weren't just the best high school in (Pennsylvania), we were the best team in the nation. So I was starting to feel pretty good about it.

■ ■ ■

LOU MCCULLOUGH
Defensive coordinator

Zelina: A comment about the coaching staff?

McCullough: I was never on one that was better. I think the great thing about OSU is its tradition. I coached at Iowa State in 1958, ten years before our national championship season at Ohio State, that was called the Dirty Thirty. And that's the team that John Cooper played on.

Zelina: Is that right? And you coached on that team ...

McCullough: Yes, I recruited John Cooper. He played for a friend of mine at a little high school just outside of Knoxville, Tennessee. And I took John with me to Iowa State. John always wanted to be a coach and he was a very good student. And a good football player. Really knew football and didn't make many mistakes. ... That football team we had in 1968, it was not the best defensive football team we had, because it only had one year of experience. ... *(Pause.)* I'll never forget that pass as long as I live. I'm sitting next to Lou Holtz and I can see it.

Zelina: What pass?

McCullough: That pass against Illinois. We were leading 24-0 at halftime. We came out the second half and fumbled and goofed up and screwed around and really didn't do anything until that pass they threw to you. And when we

threw that one and that defensive back broke coverage and you went right down the middle and caught it, and ol' Rex is knocked out on the sideline. Mace came in and threw the pass. That was probably one of the biggest plays we had that season. But I'll tell you something. Before the 1968 season started, if you remember the year before, Purdue beat the living daylights out of us. Hugh Hindman and I came out of the press box just before the half, and we got to the elevator and got downstairs and stood between the goalposts, they scored 14 points. And I said to Hugh, "I don't believe Woody would throw the ball two minutes before the half." Well, they beat us 41-6. So that summer I got a copy of all of Purdue's games and I made a film of their seven best passes against two different defenses similar to what we played. And their seven best runs. And of course they had Leroy Keyes and Mike Phipps. And I sent that around to our first and second teams and our three-deep linebackers. To Dirk Worden and Mark Stier and different ones. And then starting in July I gave them a test. Every player on our defense, I sent them a test on what we'd do in this formation and that formation. And I tell you, nobody was any better informed than we were against Purdue—13-0, and that really started us on our season.

Zelina: I've talked to a lot of guys on the defensive side of the ball and they said there was never a game that they were not prepared for. And they told stories about you running those darn sprints after practice and running them to the fence.

McCullough: But we were in better shape than any team we played.

Zelina: That's right. But to a man they said when the game came, Lou McCullough had us prepared. There was not a game that we weren't prepared for.

McCullough: And that summer, I met with Dirk Worden and Mark Stier and the rest of the LBs. I had six linebackers and I think John Muhlbach came, too. We met three hours in the morning and then we had lunch. Then we had three hours in the afternoon. We did that and I quizzed them and quizzed them, and they were smart. They just knew what Purdue was going to do. So that and the testing and the film really got us off to a great start.

Zelina: Did you have a feeling from a talent standpoint that we might be pretty good in 1968?

McCullough: No, because we had such a lousy season the year before.

Zelina: But you won the last four games of the season the year before.

McCullough: Still, you just don't know how young players are going to react. ... I'll tell you something else about that season. And this is the truth. When I went there, Coach Hayes would pick thirty-three players and he took what he wanted. He took twenty-four of the best thirty-three for offense and said, "Here, the rest is for the defense." Remember, he used to have the coaches write critiques at the end of the spring practice and at the end of the season on all the players. I've got the critique right here if you want to see it. I've got it right here in my folder. I told him if you ever want to see a championship contender you're going to have to start giving us some players on defense. We cannot win with the players that you let us have on defense. We went round and round. Finally, Woody said, "All right, you SOB. I'll tell you what we'll do. Next year I'll take one and you take one, and I'll take one and you take one." I said, "Will you remember that?" This is true. So the next year we start. So he picks Rex Kern. See, Rex had played defense and offense in high school. So when he did that, that gave me (Mike) Sensibaugh. You understand. The next choice he took (John) Brockington and that gave me Jack Tatum. Jack was a heck of a runner in high school. So that's how I got Jack Tatum and he got Brockington. We went right down the line until he got his eleven and I got my eleven. And after that it didn't matter too much. But until we did that, we just got whatever was left, and I'm serious. So that helped us. ... See, it's much easier to teach young people defense than it is offense.

Zelina: Why do you think that is?

McCullough: Shoot, offensive assignments! Let's say you're a tackle and you come up to the line of scrimmage and you've got a gap and you've got this, and if this man moves here and there's two men in your gap, you've got to take this one or you've got to make a call. Well, you can shift defenses, you see. We used to shift defenses at OSU. So it made it easier on

defense. ... The thing about that team was everybody liked everybody. You didn't have any bitching to amount to anything and they got together and got a taste of winning. And it was after the Illinois game that I thought we were going to win. See, Illinois was smart. They were content to make five, six yards a play and keep the ball. And we did some crazy things. And they did something very unusual; they made three straight two-point conversions after their TDs. But you have to have some games like that that you win.

Zelina: Going into summer practice, you still had some good senior leadership like Dirk Worden until he got hurt.

McCullough: Let me tell you about Dirk Worden. Dirk was about as tough as we had. He was smart. He met with us in the summer.

Zelina: There were a lot of good players on that defense like Paul Schmidlin, Brad Nielsen. Bill Urbanik gave you some size and quickness on that line.

McCullough: Nielsen and Urbanik were outer-space people. Old Bill Urbanik, when I'd look at him, he'd almost cry. He scared me to death with that look he had. And Nielsen, I knew he was crazy. But you know what? You've got to know who you could talk to like that and who you can't. If you said that to Schmidlin, he'd be really offended. It was really enjoyable to coach those guys. They were enjoyable people.

Zelina: Coach, what was your defensive philosophy in 1968?

McCullough: My defensive philosophy was this and it was always this: We will always be in better shape than anybody we play. And we will use multiple defenses. I used to coach offensive backs at many different places and I coached the pass offense. And I knew that multiple defenses and shifting into defenses gave the offense problems. So that's what we did. We used a 4-3 and a 5-3, which was the Oklahoma, and a 6-3. Now what that meant was, anytime we called a '3, everybody on defense knew that we were in a three-deep. So when we called a 6-1 or 4-1 or 5-1, that meant we were in a free safety, man to man. And we put in the 60 defense which was really the Notre Dame defense and we put it in to stop the run. The first thing you have to do is stop the run, even if you have to put in a truck. You got to be able to stop the run first, ya got me? We used to play Ara Parseghian when he was at Northwestern, and he used to tear up our Oklahoma defense. But when we went to the Split-Six, he wouldn't make a yard. So by shifting defenses that meant now their QB and their offensive backfield coach had to get ready for three defenses, not just one. Now that really helped us. We didn't have too much because we coordinated everything. We simplified it yet we had multiple defenses. ... I think we wouldn't have won as much as we did without multiple defenses.

Zelina: And you had the talent and the quickness to have the ability and the versatility to call those multiple defenses.

McCullough: Well, when you have Jack Tatum as your monster man and you have Ted Provost and Sensibaugh at safety and Timmy Anderson at the corner and Stillwagon and Adams and Stier in the middle, they were all smart. And I haven't even talked about our defensive ends yet. I recruited Dave Whitfield and Mark Debevc; all those guys were smart and they were good people. See, I recruited Dave Whitfield, Tim Anderson. Sensibaugh and Ted Provost. Provost was from Navarre, Ohio, if you remember. And Tim Anderson was from West Virginia, and I thought I'd never get Woody off the mountain up there. I took him up there to see (Anderson). ... But where are you going to get three QBs like Rex Kern, Maciejowski and Sensibaugh — on the freshman team? Florida really battled us for Sensibaugh.

Zelina: Sensibaugh was just inducted into our Hall of Fame. You know he is still the career leader in interceptions at OSU?

McCullough: He must have been a good one, because he had more footballs in his home than anybody else! His daddy and I were real good friends.

Zelina: What do you remember about the Michigan game, Coach?

McCullough: Well, the next game we worked on after the Purdue game was Michigan. We coaches really set our sights on them. We started preparing for them. I figured we'd whip them. I've got the Purdue game ball and the Michigan game ball right upstairs in my

trophy room. But I just felt we'd beat Michigan, and number one, I felt that physically and mentally that we would beat them. ... One philosophy we had, I always had this philosophy as a coach since I started coaching and that is —and people make this mistake and I've seen them make it and make it and make it—is you have to get to the quarterback some way in the first five minutes of the game. See, Esco Sarkkinen did our scouting, and the only game that he was with us was the Michigan game because he was always out scouting our next opponent. Anyway, the first question I'm going to ask him was how can we get to the quarterback. He might say, "Well, we can do this, this and this." Or he might say, "Well he's going to be tough, because he can really run." That was the next question I'd ask him. "Can the quarterback run? Can he run out of trouble or can he run the option?" So when we found out these things we set our defenses, if you remember, to get to the quarterback some way in the first five minutes. Against Purdue, there's a picture in the book where Phipps is about three feet off the ground with Tatum hitting him. Well, we had a Fire game on and Jack ripped him. Phipps went out of the game and when he came back in, there were four or five times when he could have run for ten or fifteen yards, but he was looking for Tatum. So people who let a quarterback sit back there and beat you to death, they're crazy. So we tried our best, and if we couldn't get to him, then our next rule was this: We're going to sacrifice something, a 5-yard pass or something, we're going to sacrifice something percentage-wise to get the quarterback. And we never played cat and mouse like a lot of people do. We played line and killing. Don't let him stand around! Hit him as hard as you can! And so that helped us a lot.

Zelina: So, against Michigan we put it on them pretty good in the second half. Remember at the end of the game, after our last touchdown when we went for two points instead of one?

McCullough: Well ... that's too bad!

Zelina: Any stories?

McCullough: I think the greatest asset Coach Hayes had was his hard work. When I took over his defense, I didn't even meet with Coach Hayes.

Zelina: You didn't?

McCullough: No, no, Coach Hayes met with the offensive coaches every morning out at the North Facility and I met with the defensive coaches at St. John Arena.

Zelina: God, you were lucky.

McCullough: Oh, I know! When I was on offense, we used to stay up until twelve o'clock, one o'clock, Saturday nights, Sunday nights, after the games, in the summer and we wasted a lot of time. So I made up my mind as the defensive coordinator, I told our coaches, "We're going to stop at ten o'clock. If we can't get it done by ten o'clock, that's it." And we did. So the offense, they said, "When you leave, make a lot of noise so Woody knows you're leaving. So we'd walk by the conference room and we'd talk really loud, you know. And if I'd stay until twelve o'clock, he'd stay until one. If I stayed until one o'clock, he'd stay until two. If I stayed until three o'clock, he'd stay until four. But if I let him know at ten o'clock, then he might let them out at ten-thirty or eleven.

Zelina: Any memories of the Rose Bowl?

McCullough: Here's a story. A lot of people don't know this. See, Dirk Worden was hurt and he couldn't play. But I put him in on defense, not in the game, but against Woody's offense. And he intercepted three passes and Woody went crazy. He came down and he said, "What are you doing playing him? If we wanted to play him, we'd be playing him first string." And I said, "Coach he wants to play defense and he's not hurting anything. He's not going to tackle anybody." Oh, he got upset and I had to put Dirk on the sideline. So on Thursday we went out with no pads, just our jerseys and helmets. Well, Mark Stier jumped up for a ball and came down on his shoulder and sprained his shoulder. It really hurt him. Now, we did not know whether Mark was going to play until thirty minutes before the ball game. Not many folks knew that. Now, when that happened, Coach Hayes went berserk. It wasn't anybody's fault. Mark just jumped and fell, you understand. We weren't hitting, we weren't doing anything. Woody got all over me. And I told him I didn't have anything to do with it. And we went back and forth. And he says, "Get Radtke ready." I said, "Coach, Radtke's been playing end all year." Well, he didn't know that

Mike had been playing end all year. I hate to say that.

Zelina: That's amazing because Radtke had some big games for us that year.

McCullough: So I had to get Mike at the Rose Bowl. We go up to the monastery, right, the day before the game, and I'll never forget, Friday afternoon late, and I've got Radtke out there and I'll never forget it as long as I live. I look up and there's the Virgin Mary statue right there, and I said to Mike, "You better pray to her, because if you make a mistake Coach Hayes is going to be on me and I'm going to be on Sark and Sark is going to be on you!" And I told Mike that "Sark isn't even going to coach you. You're going to be a linebacker." ... "A linebacker?" ... I said, "Yeah. Coach Hayes thinks you've been playing linebacker." Oh, that made Radtke mad. I had to teach him everything over again. I worked with him until nearly eleven o'clock that night, worked with him all Saturday morning. He dressed out as a linebacker for that game. But the doctors said that Mark Stier could play about forty-five minutes before the game (began) and not many people knew that. And he played a heckuva game! He popped O.J. Simpson a couple times and made him fumble."

Zelina: How did you feel when O.J. popped that 80-yard TD run?

McCullough: I felt we still were going to do all right because we had an alternate plan. If O.J. ever made one long run, we were going to put Mark Stier on him man for man. And we put it on. We called it Mirror. We went "breast to breast"—we didn't call it that—and ball to ball, right with O.J. Simpson. After he made that long run, the next time they pitched the ball to him Mark Stier hit him and he fumbled. And the next time they pitched the ball to him, Mark hit him and he fumbled. And we scored both times and that was the turning point of the game. ... Woody wrote an article, I kept it for years, in *Sports Illustrated,* and he said USC had all the stars but the stars that won the game for Ohio State were their linebackers. And of course that was the reason because we put Mark Stier on O.J. And Mark Stier did one heck of a job!

Zelina: Yeah, that was an awesome display of football.

McCullough: And twenty-four hours before that, he wasn't even going to play.

Zelina: How many years did you coach at Ohio State, Lou?

McCullough: Eight full seasons and nine spring practices.

Zelina: Was that your longest tenure at any one school?

McCullough: As a coach, yes.

Zelina: In relation to your other coaching jobs—and I'm looking for honesty; you don't have to say things just for the sake of it sounding good—how would you rate your eight years at Ohio State compared to your other experiences, if can you even do that?

McCullough: Well, see, it's all relative. When I coached Wofford College, we were a small, little school, but we started playing big-time football. And we only had 500 students. We ended up, we used to play Tennessee, Florida State, South Carolina, Auburn, schools like that. And the worst thing is that when you beat one or two of them, you understand, then nobody else wants to play you. The little schools like Furman, and Davidson and all those that have been beating your brains out for a hundred years drop out. We had some fine players at Wofford and I enjoyed it. Then we had some fine players at Wyoming because we went undefeated at Wofford and we went undefeated at Wyoming. When you start and you build up and you beat people that you're not supposed to beat, that's very satisfying. At Ohio State, when I got here, three years in the mid-1960s we weren't doing very good. And they weren't organized at all in recruiting. So, I asked Woody if I could make out his schedule on the weekends and would he please follow it? And he started doing it and I think that was a big, big, change in our recruiting. So it's fun. But you don't get the chance to win the national championship anywhere else and go to the Rose Bowl. And that makes it very special. But I enjoyed the recruiting in the state of Ohio because of the high school football coaches. Man, they knew football. There was no better areas in my years in football than Steubenville and Alliance and Niles and Canton and Massillon. That's about as good an area in those years as there was. Boy, they knew football. You didn't fool high school coaches in the state

of Ohio. They knew whether you knew football or not. So I really enjoyed the recruiting. I had to take Coach Sark out of Cleveland because Esco never drove and his wife had to drive him up there. So Coach Hayes asked me who'd I like to hire and I said Larry Catuzzi. And so we hired Larry, and boy, that made a difference. And we didn't have much contact with the Catholic schools and that's where the football players were. If you gave me the football players in the state of Ohio in my nine years and you let me take them out of the Catholic schools, I'd win the national championship nearly every year.

Zelina: I'd agree with that, because I came out of a Catholic school back then and there was a tremendous amount of great football players that I knew of then. So, anyway, your take on the 1968 team?

McCullough: We had a lot of good football players but not too many great ones, you understand. And you could count on them. They worked as a unit and everything gelled. I tell you the best football player I ever coached was Jim Stillwagon. Because he worked every day from his freshman year until the day he left. He gave you a hundred percent. I mean he really worked. See, not many people knew about him. I got him off a little eight-millimeter film. He was in a prep school and I wouldn't let anyone else have the film. He had good parents; most of the people on that team had good parents. So they had something that you just don't get together, just maybe once in a lifetime.

■ ■ ■
LOU HOLTZ
Defensive backs

Zelina: What was your first impression at Ohio State with the quality of athletes you were working with in the defensive backfield?

Holtz: I didn't know before we started spring practice because, number one, we didn't have a lot of numbers and three of the guys that they gave me in the defensive secondary never played there before. Mike Sensibaugh was a quarterback, Tatum obviously was a running back, and Timmy Anderson was, as well. So all of sudden, Provost was a cornerback, Mike Polaski played a little bit, Art Burton was a strong safety.

Zelina: You remember this stuff don't you, Coach?

Holtz: I remember pretty good. We went out for spring practice and Coach Hayes ran predominately a straight-T an awful lot during spring ball. And it was different. We had those funny headgears on in practice and the hitting was a little bit different. I just enjoyed the guys and we hadn't come off a great year in 1967. So I really didn't know what to expect. I felt we had good athletes and they were good kids and I was anxious to see what would happen.

Zelina: When did you get a feeling that what you had to work with was ... would turn out as exciting as they were?

Holtz: First of all, about the second day I noticed Jack Tatum. And I noticed him because I had this Triple-Butt drill *(which, dear reader, Mike Polaski defined for you in the Michigan chapter. Were you paying attention?)* We did the Triple-Butt and it really got you in the habit of how to roll your hips, *et cetera,* and we became pretty good at it. I'll say that.

Zelina: What was your opinion of the coaching staff the one year that you were here?

Holtz: When I was there, I really wasn't a real popular pick by the staff because the only person I knew a little bit was Esco Sarkkinen. So I was selected and they moved Earle Bruce to the offensive line. He had been working with the secondary and that didn't set well with Lou McCullough. I was really impressed with (Bill) Mallory. Liked him very, very much. I shared a room with him and an office and we roomed together on the road. And of course Sark was just totally different. He had been there forever. George Chaump came in about the same time I did and we became very good friends. But, you know I'm from Ohio and my family ... and (still) it was all new to me. It was new and it was unique and it was a very special experience for me.

Zelina: Especially coming from East Liverpool. Now, getting into the season, your first test for your defensive backfield was quite a test going against SMU.

Holtz: Well, I remember that SMU opened

up the week before we did. And they opened up with Auburn. They had a quarterback down there by the name of Chuck Hixson. Levias and Richardson were wide receivers. I went down to scout the SMU-Auburn game. And SMU beat Auburn at Auburn.

Zelina: Not an easy thing to do.

Holtz: No, it wasn't, and it was obvious that they could throw the ball and they spread 'em out. And Woody, he didn't work much on SMU. That was an exhibition game. I'm looking at them, and they got people spread out all over the lot and all we're looking at is a straight-T. So I was somewhat concerned. So we come back and they throw the ball 76 times and gain over 400 yards. We had five or six interceptions, and after the game Coach Hayes said, "Your guys did a good job." And I thought, My God, they completed over 40 passes and gained 476 yards, and he thought that was a good job? I thought, this is going to be an easy job. But we had a lot of interceptions and that was the game that just before the half when Rex Kern waved off the punter on fourth down and scrambled for a first down. We won the game 35-14, but by the same token when I looked at it, we really did some good things in the secondary. We had a number of sacks and a lot of them were coverage sacks. And so when I looked at how well we covered and some of the mistakes we made, I felt we had a chance of being pretty good even though we gave up a lot of yards. We did some good things for the first game, and we could improve on them.

Zelina: And you were working with a young bunch, too.

Holtz: We were working with a young group but they were very talented. Not only that, we had pretty good talent (elsewhere). You know, Mark Debevc had started out in the secondary and we moved him to a drop end. And we had Whitfield at the rush end. Then we had Stillwagon at middle guard; he was awfully good. And Schmidlin was one tackle. And of course we lost Dirk Worden, and Doug Adams came in and took his place. And the other linebacker was Mark Stier. But it was obvious that we had some pretty good talent there. That summer, prior to the season, we were down listening to Billy Maxstead. And Hugh Hindman was there and we're having a good time and

Hugh said, "You won't be this happy when Purdue gets hold of us." They had Keyes and Fleming, and Phipps was their quarterback. And I remember making the comment ... and I said, "We'll shut them out."

Zelina: Is it true that you had a hundred-dollar bet with Hugh?

Holtz: Yeah. What happened was we're down there and I said we'd shut out Purdue. Hugh said, "I'll bet you a hundred dollars." I said, "I'll bet you!" So we wrote it out on a napkin, and I signed it and Hugh signed it. So now our third game we play Purdue. I think they were No. 1 in the country, averaging about 43 points a game.

Zelina: That's right.

Holtz: What happened in the first half was we moved the ball pretty good. They moved it pretty good. But they wound up with a turnover or a penalty or something that prevented them from scoring. So we go in at halftime with the score tied 0-0. They played Leroy Keyes both at running back and wide receiver. And they played two wideouts to the same side. So we put in a coverage that no one had ever seen. One was called Robber coverage. Now, they ran two patterns. They sent both receivers down and they both turned out. Then they sent the inside man to the flat and hooked the other guy. And they read your strong safety. So on the snap of the ball, we read pass. Jack Tatum who looked like he was going to have the flat, would take off and run underneath the out cut. Provost would then position himself to intercept the curl cut. Sensibaugh would come over top to guard anything deep. On the second play of the second half, we put in this coverage and they threw an out cut. Jack Tatum broke underneath it and I mean he's going to score and he drops the ball. So they came back a couple plays later, and now they ran the short cut to the flat and curl. Once again, Jack Tatum took off underneath the out cut and they threw the curl, and Ted Provost was sitting there waiting, picked it off and ran in for a touchdown.

Zelina: And that was the Robber call, right?

Holtz: That was the Robber call. We should have intercepted the previous pass, but they only ran two patterns a lot there. And so we had it that no matter which one they ran,

either Tatum would intercept it or Provost would. And we would false-key them. And once Provost intercepted and ran it back, they lost confidence in their keys and in what they were doing. And then Stillwagon intercepted a pass and brought it back deep. And then Long ran it in for a TD. He came in when Kern got hurt. That was a great victory. And the thing I remember vividly was I had a lot of people down there to come help and watch the game. And at seven o'clock Woody had us in the office breaking down film. So, so much for the celebration.

Zelina: It was amazing how hard he had everybody working. ... What happened to the bet?

Holtz: When I left Ohio State, Hugh Hindman gave me a check for one-hundred dollars and wrote a poem about it. And I still have it somewhere. It hung on the wall for a lot of years. When I left they had a little party for me and Hugh had it framed and put a little rose on it.

Zelina: What about that Illinois game?

Holtz: Jim Valek is the coach. Now, Jim Valek is the godfather of my youngest son, Kevin. I coached at South Carolina with Jim Valek. I knew him well and he was having a terrible year. Illinois was having a bad year. We go out there and we're ahead 24-0 at halftime. We go in at halftime and we're not having any problems at all on defense. We come out the second half and I'll never forget, they scored three touchdowns, three two-point conversions and I don't think they threw three passes. They kept running off tackle to the short side of the field and we're rotated to the wide side of the field. And we're expecting them to throw the ball playing catch up. And I've never seen a comeback like that without throwing the ball.

Zelina: They widened their splits too, didn't they?

Holtz: Yeah, they did that. Then when they scored to tie it up 24-all, they got all excited. Then Kern got hit and got hurt, and Maciejowski came in and hit you down the middle. It was a big play, and then Otis scored. In any event we won the game and that was a big win—to come back on the road like that.

Zelina: What about Michigan State?

Holtz: They had a pretty good football

team. They scored late in the game, but really we didn't play real well. I remember Coach Hayes got a little mad at halftime.

Zelina: And Wisconsin?

Holtz: Coach Hayes liked to take us to the campus early. I remember being on campus and they had a sit-in and took over the administration building. We pounded them quite decisively. It wasn't much of a contest.

Zelina: Our first game on artificial turf, though.

Holtz: I remember going in at halftime, and their cheerleaders had those red and white sweaters with stripes going up and down. I'll never forget a cute, blonde cheerleader cussing us out. ... Then we went to Iowa.

Zelina: Right.

Holtz: It was a cold, miserable day and they had a great fullback the year before by the name of Sullivan that got hurt and couldn't play. Podolak was their tailback. They had a good football team and they played pretty well. But we played a great offensive game that game.

Zelina: And now we're up to Michigan.

Holtz: They had that little quarterback, Brown, and the big tight end, Mandich. Ron Johnson was their tailback and he was a good one. They had won, like, eight in a row. The thing I remember about that was early in the game we sent Jack Tatum on a blitz and he hit Brown from the blind side that really set the tempo for the game. It was back and forth. The winner was going to go to the Rose Bowl and everything else. Gee, we just dominated. Our offense played so great and defensively we did great.

Zelina: Yeah, we went into the locker room at halftime leading 21-14. The defense played a magnificent game the second half, too.

Holtz: Yeah, we did that. They asked Coach Hayes why he went for two (after the last touchdown of the 50-14 victory) and I'll never forget his response. He said, "Because they wouldn't let me go for three." ... Now we're on our way to the Rose Bowl.

Zelina: Bound for Pasadena.

Holtz: I remember I was in charge of the rooming list. When the wives came out, they roomed with their husbands. The day they

came out we were going out to Sunset Strip to have dinner — the whole staff, because the wives came out. And I was in charge of the rooming list. I was also duty officer. I got tied up in traffic so bad I couldn't get back. So Tiger Ellison was the only one who didn't go. I called him and asked him if he would make room check for me. Well, he said, "Yes." So what happened was, Coach Hayes saw Tiger making room checks and got mad because he thought Tiger was just too nice of a guy. So Woody got mad and said, "I'll make them" and asked, "Where's Lou?" Tiger said, "He's down on Sunset Strip." Well, Woody didn't wait for an explanation about how we got tied up and that I had every intention of being there. So Woody goes and makes the room check with his old list — and that's the day the wives came in. And he walked in on some players with their wives. Oh, he was so upset it was unbelievable! ... There was something with Tim Anderson. Tim thought I was on him too much and he was going to go home three days before the Rose Bowl. And I told him to go home. We didn't need him. And I don't remember what it was about, but I do remember that he was mad. But he wasn't half as mad as I was. Anyway we worked it out and he played a great game in the bowl game. He and Tatum played a great game.

Zelina: Relate the story about your conversation with Woody at halftime when you came down from the press box.

Holtz: We got into an argument over the best way to defend O.J. Simpson. You know Coach Hayes can be a little adamant.

Zelina: Oh, you think?

Holtz: Yeah, I just think. It was in the second quarter and USC had first down-and-10 from their own 20-yard line. I remember O.J. took a pitchout going to his left and cut up inside. We didn't stay behind the ball and he cut back behind the backside corner and turned it up and went 80 yards. And Coach Hayes got mad at halftime. He said , "Why did O.J. go 80 yards?" I said, "Well, that's all he needed! He could have gone 90 if he wanted. The only thing that could have stopped him was the Pacific Ocean." We were behind 10-0 and really came back and made a nice drive just before the half to tie it up 10-all. And then we came out the second half and dominated until the end when they caught a pass when actually Polaski intercepted it but their guy jumped on top of him and the ref ruled a simultaneous catch for a touchdown. It was a terrible call. Instead of 27-10, it wound up 27-16.

Zelina: You were only with us one year, Coach ...

Holtz: I was there the following spring, too, and it looked like we were going to have a great football team. Then the job at William and Mary opened up in July and I knew that you didn't get many chances to be a head coach. And the only reason that I was going to have it at William and Mary was because the people there knew me. I really didn't want to go and my wife didn't want to go but it was the only chance I thought I might have to be a head coach. So I took it and went.

Zelina: Well, the timing was good for you to be with us that one season and you did have a tremendous effect on us, Coach. The guys spoke so highly of you. You were a fiery little motivator who was dedicated and loved the game and the guys that you coached felt that.

Holtz: I really enjoyed it as an assistant coach and the first practice we had in spring. And this was when Woody, I think, felt I was going to be all right. We had a practice and the first play I was trying to get the defensive backs to run to the ball. And I even got up there and pushed the pile back and it was on film. Those guys, we had a special relationship with them and I'll never forget, and this really meant a lot to me: On Halloween night they all got together and came over to our house trick-or-treating with false faces on. Just little things like that. But it was great as an assistant coach. You could have a wonderful relationship with them. You could talk with them, laugh, joke and spend time with them and I really enjoyed it.

Zelina: The guys talked about how you had them over to your house.

Holtz: I would always bring them over on Thursday night and we would visit and talk about different things that we had to do and just get everybody to know one another better. Plus, you know, it was nice for my children and the wives. You know, we were like a family. We really were. You'd be on them all week but

then on Thursday, that's the time you want to build their confidence about what we had to do on Saturday. They were a fun group.

Zelina: You have a remarkable coaching record. I wondered with this team and other great teams that you coached, you could have great athletes but you needed something else, a chemistry.

Holtz: Absolutely. You know, I wasn't there the year before. But in spring practice we had a guy named Nick Roman. Now Nick was more of a veteran, and sort of knew everything. And then he got injured and couldn't play and a guy named Mark Debevc came in and took his place. You know you had all these talented people, but they also liked the game and liked to compete. It was just fun to be around. You know, John Muhlbach, a 190-pound center, and whatever else the case may be. We had the two big offensive tackles, but there was just great chemistry. The players just really loved to compete and I thought Coach Hayes did a tremendous job to take a group of young people and have the aspirations that he had for that team. But, it was the combination of everything else. Good athletes, very sound fundamentally, Coach Hayes' staff always emphasized blocking and tackling and understanding what you're doing. And we had so many big plays. You made a bundle of them, Jankowski did, Jan White did, Jim Otis.

Zelina: That was the first time in a while that Woody really had versatility in the offense, and with George Chaump's help ...

Holtz: I think George Chaump made a tremendous contribution. You know, we went to the I-slot and we threw the ball more. We used your versatility. We ran you on the counter, we ran you on the option coming back. We ran the iso (isolation)—option and throwing the ball. We just had a lot of talent. The other thing is, we had a lot of young players beat out returning starters. You beat out Gillian at wingback. Bill Long was beat out as the starting quarterback. And yet, no one complained. All they wanted to do was win. I think it was a combination of those things that enabled it to be special.

Zelina: How about some stories about Woody? Being there for just one year, did you get anything from being around Coach Hayes?

Holtz: Oh, absolutely. He influenced me more than anybody else I've ever been around as a coach. His commitment to excellence, his standards, his beliefs, his emphasis on fundamentals. ... There were a couple stories.

Zelina: Share them with me.

Holtz: My first staff meeting. I came up from the south, you know. My family's still there. It's snowing. My wife bought me a coat before I left. It's stolen at breakfast that morning. I walk into the staff meeting. I smoked a pipe then. I still do. Somebody said I better put it out "because Coach Hayes will make you swallow it." So Coach Hayes comes in and sees me smoking a pipe and he said, "What are you doing?" I said, "I'm enjoying my pipe." And he said, "You can't work for Paul Brown because Paul Brown says anybody that smokes a pipe is lazy and complacent." Well I said, "That's why you're smarter than Paul Brown because you don't believe that!" And I smoked the pipe the whole time I was there. ... But at that first staff meeting, he got mad and he threw the projector through the window, through the glass-door window there. From then on, it was chained to the table. He claimed it was chained so nobody could take it away. I think Dick Larkins probably chained it. In any event, there was a near fist fight between Coach Hayes and an assistant coach. It had to be broken up. It had to do with academics. And I walk out of there and I'm thinking, What in the world have I gotten myself into? Not knowing anything about it. But, the more you're around him, it was amazing. ... And you go recruiting. When you go recruiting, good Lord knows, you never know what he's going to talk about. He may talk about the atomic bomb for four hours and not talk to the young man about football or anything else. But, he was just a special, caring guy. He really and truly cared.

EPILOGUE
In their own words: If you only knew what it meant . . .

Through my association with the Ohio State football program, I met the finest and most loyal people in the world. Even though I do not see my teammates as much as I would like, we always pick up right where we left off. Our team does not need name tags at our reunions. The relationships I developed at Ohio State with my coaches and teammates have been invaluable to me.

Likewise, the support each and everyone of us experienced from the greatest football fans in the country certainly played a large part in our consistency and in our success. As I continued my football career in the National Football League, I would never experience this type of fan loyalty and support again.

Anyone who reads this book will understand why the spectacle of a Buckeye weekend (especially when it includes our national championship team) is so precious to all of us.

You can't be in business, you can't teach school, you can't do anything without a few stumbling blocks along the way. And the people that are successful, I think the only thread between success and failure is the fact that successful people never know when to quit. They don't quit, they can't quit. There are lots of times when the same people want to quit but they can't quit because of all this training and doing it one way.

You know, we used to kid around and said there's only two ways of doing things, the wrong way and Woody's way. Woody was a hardhead. Woody would make us do things we didn't always want to do. I don't know if there was one player on that team that played the whole time and didn't get mad at Woody and didn't think that some of the things he did were not always fair. But you look back, and there was always a reason for everything the man did. And he never let us quit. And if we didn't get our degree, it wasn't Woody's fault. It was our own.

-Jim Otis

■ ■ ■

It's great to be a Buckeye. The playing experience at OSU is the highlight of my life. The lessons learned on the football field are consistent with the lessons learned in real life. Woody said, "They may beat me but they'll never outwork me." Hard work does pay off.

Woody also used to say, "It's not that the All-American never got knocked down, but the All-American would never stay down." Perseverance always pays off in the end. The final lesson was that proper fundamentals can overcome raw talent. Our offensive line would work on the same fundamentals day after day — proper stance, double-team block, drive blocks, *et cetera*. This allowed us to work as a unit and led to the national championship in 1968.

In summary, hard work, perseverance and teamwork were the lessons learned. These are the same traits that I try to exhibit in my business career. As I said, it's great to be a Buckeye.

Finally, I'd like to mention my friend and teammate, Rufus Mayes. He died at an early age, but he was a great tackle and friend to all. His hard work made our offensive line the success it was in 1968.

-Dave Foley

■ ■ ■

t's been thirty years since the 1968 OSU football team won the national championship. I think I can speak for the rest of my teammates in stating that the "Experience of 1968" was one of the major events of all of our lives. It remains today a tremendous source of pride for everyone on this team.

From a personal standpoint, there is no question that the 1968 season has had a profound impact on my development. Hardly a day has passed by in all the ensuing years that I've not at some point thought back to that time — the relationships that existed on that team, the great personalities, the accomplishments achieved through hard work, dedication and teamwork. It was truly a great learning experience, one which we all can draw strength and guidance from. I don't believe it is an overstatement to say the "Experience of 1968" played a major role in defining who I am as a person. I think most of my teammates feel the same way.

In reflecting on those days, I would be remiss if I didn't acknowledge the huge support from the most loyal fans to be found anywhere. After all these years, that season remains vivid in the memories of so many. The 1968 team

has been the object of an almost unending amount of adoration, not just from the fans in the state of Ohio, but from those scattered clear across the U.S. That season meant and obviously still means a heck of a lot to a great deal of people.

I'd also like to thank The Ohio State University for a great education and the opportunity to represent such an extraordinary institution on the playing field.

The 1968 season was a tremendous accomplishment. The OSU football team won the national title on the field largely because of the efforts of so many. Outside the lines, there was our great coaching staff — strong men, dedicated, tireless workers who left lasting impressions on a lot of young lives; the OSU Athletic Department; the OSU faculty; the "Best Damn Band In The Land"; our training and medical staffs; the cheerleaders; the academic counselors. The list goes on and on.

The "Experience of 1968" created bonds, memories and friendships for a lifetime. I'm sure that my teammates feel as I do: We are a unique lifelong fraternity. We're as close as family and all of us are truly honored and grateful to have been a part of it! We also understand that we didn't do it alone. To Buckeyes everywhere—past, present, and future—THANKS!

-Dirk Worden

■ ■ ■

appreciate this chance to write a few personal words of thanks for the opportunity the university gave to me and what it has meant to me over the years.

I can honestly say that seldom does a day go by that someone does not mention something to me about Ohio State, whether it be about football or not. Since I have been a high school teacher and coach for 28 years, most often those comments deal with football and most often with Woody. The things I learned playing and coaching for him I still use every day, both in the classroom and on the field, but more importantly, just dealing with people in everyday life. I am sure that experience has opened doors for me even more than I realize.

I have said many, many times I feel I have

been a very lucky person throughout my life. Great family, great friends, went to a great high school, played with great players and for great coaches. That, of course, just continued in Columbus. I feel very blessed to have gone to Ohio State and to become a Buckeye when I did. Same great family, more great friends, a lot more really great players and coaches. I was just in the right place at the right time.

The friends that we made, the things we learned and the experiences at Ohio State can never, ever be taken away from us. In particular, I truly want to thank Woody, Earle Bruce, Lou McCullough and Hugh Hindman for the opportunity that they gave a short, slow, fat kid from Canton. I also want to say a big thank you to the university in general for a great education and a great experience. I don't know how it could have been any better.

-Jim "Pork" Roman

To have been a part of the 1968 national championship team is still my fondest memory. My thanks to The Ohio State University, the coaching staff, medical and equipment staffs, the Columbus media and, above all, my teammates for the opportunity, training, care, support and friendship that has been shared throughout the years. I also want to thank my "biggest fans," Hugh and Betty Sensibaugh, for their support, direction, and love. (Hugh is no longer with us as of October 1997).

A special thanks to our Buckeye fans, most dominant in central Ohio, but believe me, they are everywhere! To be remembered after thirty years is one thing, but to have the opportunity to relive a season with you is truly something special. Thanks for your support and dedication!

And last but not least, a special "thank you" to Steve Hayes for sharing his father with us. I am honored to have had the opportunity to experience Woody Hayes.

-Mike Sensibaugh

Reflecting on one's past, it is hard to comprehend a national championship was won thirty years ago. Yet, as I live my life, there are many friends, family members, coaches, business associates and important others that are owed a debt of gratitude.

The fans who never forgot the team and its accomplishments, The Ohio State University for the honor to earn a degree and participate in collegiate athletics, the coaches for their effort to teach life and football lessons, the alumni for the summer jobs and career head starts, and especially three families I could never repay for their contribution.

The Hayes family and coach Hayes' importance in life's direction become more evident as each day passes. The Sarkkinen family and Sark, my family and substitute father during those years of maturation at OSU.

And, the most important facet of my life, my family. A mother and a father instilling old country values and allowing me to know I had a family history and a tradition to maintain. My parents' work ethic provided the family atmosphere to strive for personal improvement and accept only my best effort. A brother and a sister who were always there when I needed emotional support. Uncle Virg, for taking me to practices and games when my father could not, and for being a friend all my life.

These few paragraphs are a humble attempt to offer thanks in a public forum that I may never have again. To all, I owe so much.

"How firm thy friendship, Ohio." These words ring through my life and live in my memories.

-Nick Roman

As a high school two-time All-American athlete, I had the offer of attending more than one hundred colleges across this nation. Fortunately, Ohio State University offered one of those opportunities.

From my first contact with coach Woody Hayes, his staff and a subsequent visit to this

Big Ten campus, it was clear to me that OSU would be my choice. It was solidified even more following Coach Hayes' visit to my school and meeting my parents.

For me, four years at OSU was much more than just an academically enriching experience. Although today I still work in the professional field of my major studies, it laid other foundations as well.

I have built a lifetime of friendships from contacts with other athletes and students. Memories of taking the field before 85,000 people, scoring my first touchdown in Ohio Stadium or winning a Rose Bowl and national championship are all immeasurable. However, something even more intrinsic occurred. I learned about self-discipline, loyalty, perseverance and goal achievement. These are all very positive character traits which guide me today and will guide me into the future.

Go Bucks!

-Jan A. White

■■■

Life is a wonderful mystery, and I thank God for it. I always marvel when reflecting on the events that converged in 1968 and allowed me to play a part on this national championship team. In 1968, I was not yet twenty years old, but through the grace of God and the generosity of others I had a treasure of experience given to me.

Yes, there was the loving home providing a quality foundation and Christian values. And there were the discipline and fundamentals taught to me at good old Rogers High in Toledo.

Yet, when I arrived on The Ohio State University campus in the fall of 1966, I was a naive boy with no real concept of the world that would be opened. Though heavily recruited, I still did not understand the possibilities that would be offered me at this great university.

The entire coaching staff that greeted us was exceptional. Tough? Yes! And strongly disciplined. But they were also generous and genuinely caring. Sure, it is possible to complain about some of the tactics they used—"Send 'em back Sark, they're loafing!" Yet I cannot argue with the results, nor do I ever doubt

that they had my best interests at heart. If we were going to be winners, that meant paying the price.

I have often commented on the wealth of coaching talent that coach Woody Hayes had gathered together, as well as the athletic ability of the team. But even more significant to me was what I choose to call our "common team love." We came from diverse backgrounds and it would have been easy to find things to fight about, criticize or reject. Yet, with few exceptions, we were knit into a single unit. I know that the hard work and discipline were crucial, but there was more. The players on this team developed a true respect—a "love" for one another. We each learned to sacrifice our own wants for the good of the team. I learned, as a part of this championship team, how essential it is to work with others. I learned to overlook some of the little things that hurt me in favor of gaining a greater good for all. This lesson has served me every year since.

Was it Woody's stories? His drive? Was it the great body of coaching talent? Was it the sheer athletic skill of so many players? Was it the emphasis on the education first and then to play a game? Perhaps it was the idealism of the times, or maybe it was just the chemistry we generated. Was it the never-say-die commitment of the fans? Was it the many friendships established? It was all this and more.

I do thank God for that time. I do thank the coaches and my teammates. I thank the fans and the university for the support. I received a world-class education.

The classroom, the football field, the dorm room and the fraternity house ... each offered a stage for the finest interpersonal education this man could ask for.

Thank you, teammates! Thank you, Ohio State! May God bless!

-Paul Schmidlin

■■■

Our team was a compilation of slightly above-average athletes from winning high school programs. Our blue-collar work ethics were firmly in place before joining forces at The Ohio State University.

Woody Hayes provided the ingredients of masterful motivation, leadership and a true respect for one another. In addition, he showed us the true power of positive winning attitudes combined with focus on a common goal: winning it all!

To be part of a group of young men guided by such a talented, masterful leadership was—and thirty years later still is—the most important factor in my personal development. To realize and live the benefit of people performing far beyond their own expectations of their abilities for a common goal can only be measured now as mature successful adults.

I thank God for the lifelong friendships that were created and for that "handshake guarantee" Woody gave my dad, which ensured that his son would leave OSU with a college degree.

-R.G. "Butch" Smith

■ ■ ■

To begin, Columbus has been a unique city for quite some time. While it has big-city size, it has maintained a small-town soul. The people are good-natured and friendly. It has a large metropolitan area and population, but no major league sports franchises to date. Consequently, the community identifies very strongly with The Ohio State University and the successes of its athletic programs. I think it has been a very symbiotic relationship over the years, one that has greatly benefited both the community and the university. Support breeds success and success breeds support. The two continually feed off each other, creating a snowball effect.

Because of this intense community interest that has been generated, I am constantly amazed by the number of people who remember what our team was fortunate enough to accomplish thirty years ago. When they speak about it their memories are so vivid. They mention details about the players, coaches, the games like they were discussing something that happened three years ago instead of thirty.

When I look at the success we were fortunate to enjoy so long ago, in the perspective of what it meant to so many others and the sense of pride and the enjoyment it gave them, I take

great pride that I was a part of it. But I also realize that it didn't happen by accident. We invested a lot of time, a lot of effort, a lot of blood, sweat, and I'm sure—along the way—some tears to achieve what we did.

It was a tremendous blend of truly talented athletes complemented by a great coaching staff that was able to harness and direct the energy and ability of a young team that played with a great enthusiasm. They did a masterful job of keeping the team focused on the task at hand. Regardless of the amount of hard work they put us through to achieve that end, I look back and remember how much fun we had both on and off the field.

I don't remember the team or the coaches talking specifically about winning the national championship at any point during the season. That achievement came as a result of our willingness as a group to do the things necessary to stay focused on winning one game at a time. By doing that we became part of something that is special as a team, the university with its proud tradition and the community as a whole.

The fact that thirty years later we are still the last Big Ten team to be the undisputed national champion just makes me appreciate it more. It truly was a very special moment in time.

-Mike Polaski

■ ■ ■

I consider myself one of the luckiest people in the world to have been able to attend Ohio State and play football for the legendary Woody Hayes.

I had "once-in-a-lifetime experiences" at OSU. I'll never forget the first time I ran onto the field against SMU at the beginning of my sophomore year. The sheer volume of people and the unbelievable roar of the crowd was something I could never have imagined. Naturally, I had butterflies in my stomach.

As the football seasons progressed, I still never got used to looking up and seeing the huge sea of scarlet. Our fans were the best in the country. My parents came from New Jersey to see every home game, and I'm sure OSU football became an important part of the lives of all our families those years. We all developed some special friendships that exist to this day.

I came to respect and love Woody Hayes, his ability to pull the best from each one of us and his uncanny knack of knowing us all so well, caring deeply for "his boys." He was definitely hard on us; his wrath was something we all wanted to avoid. Our Woody stories are so numerous and funny, it's hard to believe some of the antics we got away with. Who can forget the image of Woody, hat scrunched up in his hand, jumping up and down, screaming commands at us? Yet, the discipline and the work ethic instilled in me while playing football at OSU was definitely excellent preparation for the future.

The team itself was a great group of guys. We had outstanding games and many great times together, but the march to our 1968 national championship stands out so much in my mind. We were so intense, so dedicated and so committed to winning that season. A very special group of coaches and players came together that year and accomplished something that hasn't been duplicated.

The fact that we were national champions on the field carried over to individual accomplishments off the field. Our coaches went on to excel in collegiate and professional ranks. Our players went on to become outstanding citizens who have accomplished much professionally and contributed to the world around. Woody would have liked that as much as the championship itself.

The Columbus community has given such support to OSU football over the years. I remember how everything centered on Buckeye football, how some businesses simply closed down for home games. I've been to Notre Dame, Michigan and even Nebraska football games, none of which measures up to the excitement and fan support shown us at Ohio Stadium during those years.

I'll never forget the outstanding reception and response from the community when we reconvened for our twenty-fifth national championship reunion in 1993. The celebration was overwhelming and made us all feel very special to have been a part of such wonderful tradition. I want to thank the Columbus community for treating us all so well through-

out those years.

As I prepare to send my eighteen-year-old daughter off to college this next fall, I wonder what her experience will be like. I can only hope she feels a measure of the success and has the same opportunity to partake in the same great spirit and tradition that OSU gave to me. Little did I know at the time how much it would mean to my life.

OSU football ... the Buckeyes ... Woody ... . There's not much that can compare with that type of college experience.

-Bruce Jankowski

■ ■ ■

My experience with the OSU football program had a profound influence on the quality of my life. The thrill of winning a national championship in 1968 and the life-long friendships made during those years were unbelievable.

However, the single most important thing I took away from those years was my education. I started out as a below-average student with little motivation. Coach Hayes preached to me the importance of education and eventually my grades improved. Upon graduation, Coach Hayes personally went with me to my law school interviews, and I am convinced that he was the reason I was accepted. After that, quite frankly, I was too scared to fail.

-Judge William Pollitt
Franklin County (Ohio) Municipal Court

■ ■ ■

One Moment In Time" was the theme for our twenty-fifth national championship reunion and celebration. That theme describes how special our team is. The aura and magnetism still exist today, some thirty years later.

I believe God enabled special group of very, very talented players to descend on the campus of The Ohio State University. Our 1968 team accomplished the unthinkable: a Big Ten championship, a Rose Bowl victory, an undefeated season, and the national championship.

During the late 1960s, college campuses were victimized by the Vietnam War, social unrest, racial tension and the defiance of authority. Our campus was not immune. Remarkably, our team remained focused because of the quality of players and Woody's tenacity for detail. His total awareness of the world and current events was unparalleled. Woody and our coaches worked hard to build us up, not tear us down.

How does one begin to thank his teammates, coaches, trainers, doctors, equipment personnel, brain coach, alumni, friends of Ohio State, the tens of thousands of fans, and family? It is an ominous task. In my case, words very seldom express my deepest feelings.

To my teammates, I have a deep fondness, a sense of gratitude, commitment, and thankfulness for allowing me to be your friend and teammate. You empowered and challenged me to be the best I could. THANK YOU!

To my coaches, trainers, doctors, equipment personnel, and brain coach, thank you for your direction, guidance, understanding and compassion. You kept us together for the betterment of our team.

To our alumni, friends of Ohio State, and the tens of thousands of fans, thank you for supporting, encouraging and appreciating our efforts, talent and accomplishments. We represent a great university and an unequaled athletic tradition. This is sacred to me!

To my parents, thank you for my values and your support at my athletic events. To Keith, my brother, you challenged me athletically because I tried to be like you! You were good, very good!

To my Lord, Jesus Christ, thank you for being there to lift me up when I stumble and fall short, and for the athletic talent you blessed me with.

-Rex Kern
Ol' #10

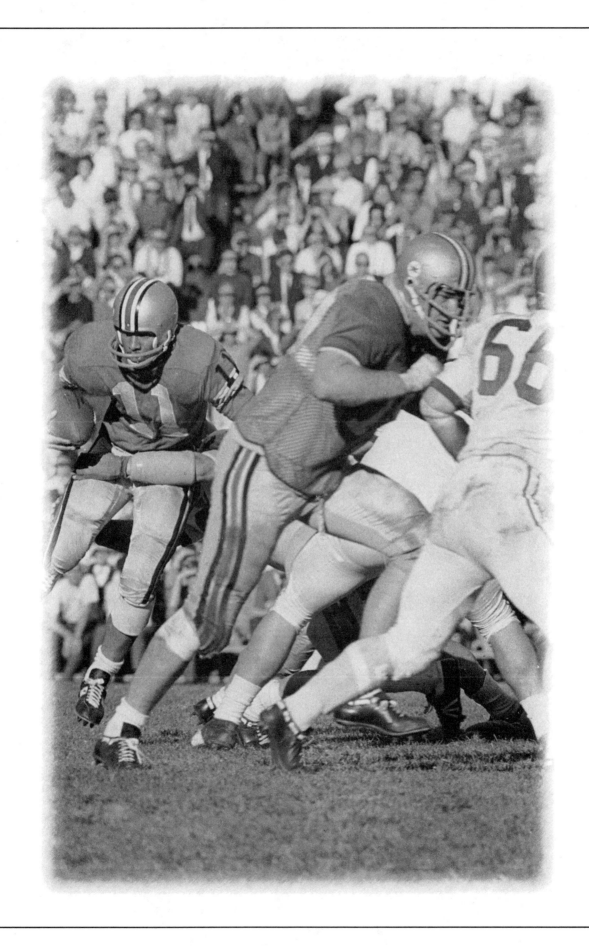

APPENDIX A
1968 Ohio State Roster

No.	Name	Pos.	Ht.	Wt.	Yr.	Hometown
63	Doug Adams	LB	6-0	215	So.	Xenia
85	Charles Aldrin	ORE	6-3	207	So.	Glenview, IL
26	Tim Anderson	DRH	6-0	194	So.	Follansbee, WV
86	Daniel Aston	DRE	6-2	208	Jr.	Cincinnati
57	Tom Backhus	ORG	5-11	207	Jr.	Cincinnati
33	Thomas Bartley	LB	5-11	198	Sr.	Springfield
19	Edward Bender	ORH	6-0	172	Sr.	Akron
48	Jay Bombach	ORH	6-1	201	Sr.	Dayton
42	John Brockington	ORH	6-1	210	So.	Brooklyn, NY
12	David Brungard	OLH	5-10	184	Jr.	Youngstown
21	Arthur Burton	LB	6-1	193	Jr.	Fostoria
75	David Cheney	OLG	6-3	230	So.	Lima
47	James Coburn	DLH	5-11	190	So.	Maumee
95	James Conroy	ORG	6-2	208	So.	Bay Village
94	Steven Crapser	DLT	6-1	216	Jr.	Columbus
36	Dick Cunningham	FB	5-10	188	So.	Portsmouth
83	Mark Debevc	DRE	6-1	210	So.	Geneva
78	John Dombos	DLT	6-0	205	So.	Garfield Hts.
66	Brian Donovan	OLG	6-3	206	So.	Columbus
90	Thomas Ecrement	DLE	6-0	195	So.	Canton
28	Gerald Ehrsam	S	6-0	194	Sr.	Toledo
70	David Foley	ORT	6-5	246	Sr.	Cincinnati
39	James Gentile	LB	6-2	210	Jr.	Poland
11	Ray Gillian	OLH	5-11	194	Jr.	Uniontown, PA
44	Horatius Greene	OLH	5-11	190	Jr.	Jersey City, NJ
51	William Hackett	LB	6-1	204	Jr.	London
65	Randy Hart	ORT	6-2	220	Jr.	Willoughby
22	Leophus Hayden	OLH	6-2	204	So.	Dayton
67	Ralph Holloway	MG	6-1	222	So.	Oberlin

No.	Name	Pos.	Ht.	Wt.	Yr.	Hometown
34	Paul Huff	FB	6-3	217	Jr.	Dover
72	Charles Hutchison	OLT	6-3	240	Jr.	Carrollton
61	Alan Jack	ORG	6-0	215	So.	Wintersville
82	Bruce Jankowski	OLE	5-11	192	So.	Fair Lawn, NJ
10	Rex Kern	QB	6-0	180	So.	Lancaster
45	Gerald King	DLE	6-3	208	So.	Columbus
81	Richard Kuhn	ORE	6-2	208	So.	Louisville
64	Ted Kurz	ORG	6-2	222	So.	Struthers
84	Edward Lapuh	DLE	6-1	198	So.	Cleveland
24	Billy Long	QB	6-1	180	Sr.	Dayton
18	Ron Maciejowski	QB	6-2	186	So.	Bedford
49	Jack Marsh	DRE	6-2	208	So.	Elyria
73	Rufus Mayes	OLT	6-5	250	Sr.	Toledo
30	Dick Merryman	K	5-8	175	Jr.	Hannibal
53	John Muhlbach	C	5-10	194	Sr.	Massillon
77	Brad Nielsen	DRT	6-3	222	Jr.	Columbus
76	Jim Oppermann	OLT	6-4	240	So.	Bluffton
35	Jim Otis	FB	6-0	208	Jr.	Celina
25	Steven Page	S	5-10	176	So.	Columbia Station
15	Mike Polaski	DLH	5-10	170	Jr.	Columbus
97	Bill Pollitt	LB	6-2	212	Jr.	Dayton
46	Ted Provost	DLH	6-3	182	Jr.	Navarre
58	Larry Qualls	C	6-0	190	So.	Dayton
43	Richard Quilling	S	6-1	190	Jr.	Celina
55	Michael Radtke	LB	6-1	200	Jr.	Wayne, NJ
52	Jim Roman	C/K	6-0	211	Sr.	Canton
89	Nick Roman	DRE	6-4	221	Sr.	Canton
59	Gary Roush	ORT	6-4	200	Sr.	Springfield
23	Kevin Rusnak	ORH	6-1	190	Jr.	Garfield, NJ
74	Paul Schmidlin	DLT	6-1	222	Jr.	Toledo
3	Mike Sensibaugh	S	6-0	187	So.	Cincinnati
17	Bruce Smith	S	5-10	150	So.	Gallipolis
50	Butch Smith	DRT	6-2	224	Jr.	Hamilton
87	Robert Smith	ORE	6-4	221	Sr.	Lakewood
91	John Sobolewski	DRE	6-1	192	Sr.	Steubenville
54	Mark Stier	LB	6-1	202	Sr.	Louisville
68	Jim Stillwagon	MG	6-0	220	So.	Mt. Vernon
69	Vic Stottlemyer	MG	6-0	200	Sr.	Chillicothe
92	John Stowe	OLE	6-2	200	Sr.	Columbus
62	Phil Strickland	ORG	6-1	217	So.	Cincinnati
37	Vince Suber	LB	6-1	186	So.	Struthers
32	Jack Tatum	LB	6-0	204	So.	Passaic, NJ
17	Robert Trapuzzano	DRH	6-0	187	Jr.	McKees Rocks, PA
71	Richard Troha	ORT	6-3	227	So.	Cleveland
79	Bill Urbanik	DLT	6-3	238	Sr.	Donora, PA
98	Charles Waugh	OLG	6-0	180	So.	Clinton

No.	Name	Pos.	Ht.	Wt.	Yr.	Hometown
41	Tim Wagner	DRH	5-10	175	So.	Columbus
80	Jan White	OLE	6-2	214	So.	Harrisburg, PA
88	David Whitfield	DLE	6-0	184	Jr.	Massillon
56	Dirk Worden	LB	6-0	198	Sr.	Lorain
16	Larry Zelina	ORH	6-0	195	So.	Cleveland

Coaching staff: Woody Hayes, head coach; Lou McCullough, defensive coordinator and linebackers; Earle Bruce, centers and offensive guards; Hugh Hindman, offensive tackles and ends; Rudy Hubbard, running backs; George Chaump, quarterbacks; Esco Sarkkinen, defensive ends; Bill Mallory, defensive tackles and middle guards; Lou Holtz, defensive backs; Glenn "Tiger" Ellison, freshmen team; Ernie Godfrey, kickers.

Support staff: Ernie Biggs, head trainer; John Bozik, equipment manager. Bob Murphy, head team physician. Jim Jones, academic coach.

Source: The Ohio State University

APPENDIX B
Team Statistics

Rushing offense	OSU	OPP
Plays	656	425
Net yardage	3025	1153
Avg. per game	302.5	115.3
Avg. per play	4.61	2.71
Touchdowns	34	12

Passing offense	OSU	OPP
Attempts	188	304
Completions	104	153
Interceptions	11	25
Net yardage	1384	1772
Avg. per game	138.4	177.2
Avg. per reception	13.3	11.6
Touchdown passes	10	9

Total offense	OSU	OPP
Total plays	847	729
Net yardage	4402	2925
Avg. per game	440.2	292.5
Avg. per play	5.19	4.01

First downs	OSU	OPP
Total	237	173
By rushing	164	77
By passing	62	85
By penalty	11	13

Interceptions	OSU	OPP
Total	25	11
Returned	21	10
Yards	209	85

Punting	OSU	OPP
Total	52	66
Yardage	1937	2567
Average	37.25	38.89

Fumbles	OSU	OPP
Total	26	32
Lost	9	16

Penalties	OSU	OPP
Total	51	43
Yards	512	425

Scoring by quarters

Ohio State	60	90	75	98	—	323
Opponents	14	44	49	43	—	150

APPENDIX C
Individual Statistics

Rusnak	1	10	0
R. Smith	1	5	0

Rushing	Num.	Yds.	Avg.
Otis	219	985	4.5
Kern	131	534	4.0
Zelina	39	338	8.6
Hayden	61	284	4.6
Brungard	66	261	3.9
Maciejowski	43	193	4.5
Brockington	45	187	4.2
Gillian	19	125	6.6
Huff	15	47	3.1
Long	7	40	5.7
Greene	5	17	3.4
Coburn	2	8	4.0
White	1	2	2.0
Kuhn	1	0	0.0
Sensibaugh	2	-2	-1.0

Scoring	TD	XP	XP2	FG	Pts.
Otis	17	—	—	—	102
Kern	8	—	—	—	48
Roman	0	21	—	5	36
Maciejowski	4	—	—	—	24
Brungard	3	—	—	—	18
Jankowski	3	—	—	—	18
Zelina	2	1	—	—	13
Hayden	2	—	—	—	12
Long	1	—	1	—	8
Provost	1	—	—	—	6
White	1	—	—	—	6
Bender	1	—	—	—	6
Polaski	1	—	—	—	6
Brockington	1	—	—	—	6
Gillian	1	—	—	—	6
Merryman	—	6	—	—	6

Passing	Att.	Comp.	Int.	Pct.	Yds.	TD
Kern	131	75	6	57.2	972	7
Maciejowski	42	25	3	59.5	387	3
Long	14	4	2	28.6	25	0
Zelina	1	1	0	100.0	0	
Brungard	1	0	0	0.0	0	0
*XP2						

Punting	No.	Yds.	Avg.
Sensibaugh	52	1937	37.25

Receiving	Rec.	Yds.	TD
Jankowski	31	328	3
Zelina	18	327	1
White	21	283	1
Brockington	7	104	0
Gillian	6	100	1
Otis	10	82	0
Hayden	4	41	1
Brungard	2	38	2
Bender	1	37	1
Kuhn	2	29	0
Rusnak	1	10	0
R. Smith	1	5	0

Punt returns	No.	Yds.	Avg.
Sensibaugh	10	93	9.3
Polaski	7	75	6.3
Zelina	9	62	6.9
Otis	1	17	17.0
Tatum	1	17	17.0
Provost	2	0	0.0

Kickoff returns	No.	Yds.	Avg.	Interception returns	No.	Yds.	TD
Zelina	9	204	22.6	Sensibaugh	5	83	0
Hayden	3	58	19.3	Provost	4	35	1
Brockington	3	53	17.6	Tatum	3	18	0
Brungard	3	43	14.3	Stier	3	9	0
Gillian	3	41	13.7	Anderson	2	0	0
Otis	2	21	11.5	Adams	2	24	0
Tatum	1	13	13.0	Burton	1	23	0
Kuhn	1	1	1.0	Polaski	1	10	0
Jack	1	0	0.0	Nielsen	1	4	0
Cheney	1	0	0.0	Debevc	1	3	0
Roman	1	0	0.0	Stillwagon	1	0	0
				Radtke	1	0	0

About the Authors

Steve Greenberg, 42, is the manager for Star/News Direct Publishing, a division of Indianapolis Newspapers Inc. The former assistant managing editor for sports at *The Indianapolis Star* and *The Indianapolis News,* he is the author of *I Remember Woody: Recollections of the Man They Called Coach Hayes* (Masters Press, September 1997), *The Minor League Road Trip* (The Stephen Greene Press/Viking-Penguin, 1990) and is working on other manuscripts, including an untitled novel tale. Greenberg has worked as a reporter and editor in the newspaper industry since 1977 and has won awards for his writing, direction of coverage and design. A graduate of Kent State University with a Bachelor of Arts degree in journalism, he is married to the former Sarah (Sally) Price and lives in Carmel, Indiana, with his wife and daughters Annie (9) and Rachel (6).

Larry Zelina, 48, is associated with the Archer-Meek-Weiler Agency in Columbus, Ohio. A member of Ohio State's "Super Sophs" of 1968, he is the former standout wingback on the 1968 national championship team. Zelina was a three-year starter for the Buckeyes, and he led the nation in punt returns in 1969. He still holds the OSU single-season record for return average (18.6 yards), which he established in 1969. He is the president of Ohio State's Varsity O Alumni Association. He was drafted by the Cleveland Browns of the National Football League in 1971, but suffered a severe, career-ending hamstring injury. This is his first book. A marketing major at Ohio State, he is married to the former Lorie Francis and lives in Worthington, Ohio, with his wife and children Michael (19), Julie (13) and Kristie (9).